Fireflies

God's Lessons on the Farm

By

Ron Stout

Copyright © 2004 by Ron Stout

Fireflies
by Ron Stout

Printed in the United States of America

ISBN 1-594676-48-8

All rights reserved solely by the author. The author guarantees all contents are original and do not infringe upon the legal rights of any other person or work. No part of this book may be reproduced in any form without the permission of the author. The views expressed in this book are not necessarily those of the publisher.

Unless otherwise indicated, Bible quotations are taken from the *New International Version.* Copyright © 1973, 1978, 1984 by International Bible Society.

www.xulonpress.com

A Special Thanks . . .

To my wonderful wife who has been such a steadfast, helpful, and loving companion. Without her extraordinary help these past few months I might still be floundering. In addition, she always deflects my apologies for becoming emotional when the Holy Spirit deals with me. In this regard I am reminded of a professional athlete who recently visited our area. While counseling a young man he had just led to Jesus, the athlete commented, "Men don't cry, Christians do."

Table of Contents

1 **BIG SKY** 9
   Is God? Or God is!

2 **FOUR SEASONS** 19
   Good News!

3 **HOWIE** 31
   New Birth

4 **GORED!** 39
   Satan Attacks!

5 **BOYSENBERRIES** 47
   The True Vine

6 **LIVING WATER** 53
   Bible Study

7 **DIVIDEND** 59
   God's Ways

8 **ELSIE** 65
   Worship

9   **THE GARDEN** **71**
     Self-sufficiency

10 **MYRTLE** **79**
     No One is Perfect

11 **PRUNING** **83**
     Group Prayer

12 **THE GIANT OAK** **89**
     The Cathedral

13 **LET'S MAKE A DEAL** **93**
     Just Praise Him !

14 **THE MOWER** **99**
     Keep on Praising Him

15 **NOAH'S ARK** **105**
     God Provides a Way

16 **THE RACCOON** **113**
     Thief in the Night

17 **CALVING** **117**
     Some Need Help

18 **THE PEAR TREE** **125**
     Fruit !

19 **TWINS** **131**
     God Knows His Own

20 **THE DAY THE LAMB DIED** **141**
     The Life is in the Blood!

21 **THE HEIFER KICKED** **147**
    Rejection

22 **APPLES, APPLES, APPLES** **153**
    Myth Dispelled!

23 **THE DOOR IS OPEN** **159**
    Nothing Happens Until It Is!

24 **HARVEST** **163**
    The Work To Be Done

25 **FIRE FLIES** **175**
    Tiny Flickers of Illumination

CHAPTER ONE

Big Sky

Is God? Or God is!

While attending a cattle seminar in Fort Collins, Colorado a number of years ago, I became acquainted with a young cowboy who was rooming next to me at the motel. We rode back and forth together to the ranch-school. Late one afternoon as we were returning from class, I looked over westward toward the Rockies and drank in the beautiful scenery. The mountains had darkened to a purple hue, the sky was a deep blue, the white clouds fluffed up high over the mountains with the sun lighting them from behind.

I casually remarked, "Isn't that sky beautiful tonight?"

He turned his head and briefly took in the sight, and then totally surprised me by saying, "No."

"Why 'no?'" I asked.

His only answer was, "You should see the sky in Montana. That's Big Sky country."

Later in life I was to spend many weeks in Montana, but at that time I had never been there, and felt that one doesn't have to be in Montana to appreciate the skies of the western

United States. One only needs to be away from the cities. There is so much air pollution around the cities that the beauty is dulled, if not completely obliterated.

At night, cities glow. There are so many bright lights that can be seen for miles away. Many years ago while I was on a Navy ship, we picked up the glow of Hong Kong over 50 miles away over the horizon. People who live in the city do not realize how the glow dulls their night vision of the sky. They are simply unable to experience the bountiful beauty of the western sky. Also folks in many areas of the United States live under a somewhat perpetual cloud cover that obscures their sky.

There is something broadening, something enriching, about walking out under a clear, dark, western sky at night. Alone. It seems to emphasize a person's smallness, his insignificance. Thoughts quite naturally turn to God.

God? Is there really a God? Is there really a super-intelligence – omniscient and divine—who is so powerful He created the entire universe? Or did it just happen? Was the universe spawned into existence by chance? How did all the stars get out there? How far do they go? Where is the end of it?

And what about mankind? Did we simply evolve, ever so gradually, over eons of time, from one-celled living organisms to what we are now? Why?

God vs. Evolution

One black night, many years ago, I walked out under the twinkling stars and pondered these questions. *It really comes down to God versus Evolution. Do we really have proof of either? There is a plethora of 'evidence,' but no solid proof. So, whatever you accept, don't you have to accept that in faith? The person who believes in God admittedly believes in faith, but doesn't the person who believes in evolution also have to believe **that** in faith? He has no* *proof, only theories and ideas, coupled with fragmented concepts that can be challenged again and again.*

Standing in the darkness I witnessed a 'falling star' shoot across the sky. I remembered my scientific background in college. I took courses in biology, comparative anatomy, physiology, histology, endocrinology, chemistry, and related fields. Never did I ever find anything that absolutely – or even convincingly – proved evolution. The comparative anatomy course was supposed to do it, but it only proved that all the species relate to each other in a close, fascinating way. Never was any proof offered to substantiate the theory that species actually *did* change to other species. As a matter of fact, it is my opinion that the anatomical relationships between species go farther toward establishing the existence of a superior intelligence, i.e. God, than they do to evolution.

But pursuing the evolution theory that I was so diligently taught in school, where does it all make sense? Or does it? Or does it have to? If mankind evolved through a course of 'natural selection,' can it continue? How? It seems that natural selection of the human race has been eliminated in many societies via the birth control pill, abortion, life-support systems with hospitals renewing life to those who would have 'naturally' died. These practices are rapidly being spread into the third world.

Looking at the moon, I remembered the television shot back in the 70's of the earth from the astronauts at the moon. The earth looked so peaceful and somewhat insignificant. Yet the truth is, mankind is in serious danger of depleting our natural resources through consumption. We are in terrible danger of experiencing global warming as a result of that consumption. We are witnessing newer diseases, such as AIDS, ravish the world's population. Production of weapons of mass destruction – biological, chemical, and nuclear – so potentially devastating that, if unleashed, could return the world to pre-historic times without the corresponding balance of nature. Perhaps the world would no longer be able to sustain life.

Where is all of this going? *Many people tell us mankind is gradually getting better, more and more civilized. Indeed! The only things that look as though they are continuing to improve are mankind's technology and standard of living.*

Question: Are we not deluding ourselves in equating a rising standard of living to moral evolution?

The abhorrent cruelties in the wars of the twentieth century fail to show any moral evolution. The atrocities were as evil as any war in history, if not worse. And now, radical Islam kills innocent people in the name of God. *In the name of God!*

And what about the peaceful world? Where is the moral evolution? *Greed, lust, avarice, deceit, dishonesty, corruption* – in government, in business, in families, even in churches and charitable organizations seems commonplace wherever one turns.

Question: Why would mankind get better? There are many old, stock answers, such as (1) to survive; or (2) to get along without violence; or (3) to do good and improve the world. Great answers, but they only lead us to the next question.

What is there in mankind's nature that would make it want to get better? That answer must be *intelligence*, an intelligence that carries with it a **conscience.** This conscience inherently displays many intangible senses – a sense of responsibility, a sense of shame, a sense of accomplishment, a sense of time – past, present, future, a sense of comprehension…in a word, **reason.**

Only mankind can really reason. Any animals that display reason do so in only a rudimentary sense. No animal can reason like a human being.

So, let's reason a little about God. Standing out under

Fireflies

the stars on a clear night is a magnificent setting to reason about God. I can most certainly recommend it. Try it! Walk out under the stars some night in the dark and quiet, and reflect on the purpose of all this.

Start off by assuming that God did create the world and mankind.

What was His purpose? Did He even have any? Did God create with no purpose in mind but His own amusement, that is, to see how long the earth could go before ultimately destroying itself? Or to see how long it would take mankind to become perfect? Do either of these motives make sense?

This only leads to more questions. Did God create people to simply turn them loose to live as they chose so He could judge them all later – rewarding and punishing each person according to the sum total of what he or she did?

Many people think so. I had an employer once who told me, "If there is a God, He will judge everyone by what he has done with what he was given." His reference was obviously to IQ, position in life, etc.

Observation. All the religions of the world, except one, are based upon the concept, and have as a common theme, "Do good and reach God."

Why do these religions exist? What is the common denominator? Could it be...is it...instinct?

There is not a day goes by on the ranch but what we observe our animals acting according to their instincts. It seems reasonable that man would do this too. I believe each and every individual who has ever lived has a soul instinct, an instinct that desires immortality. No one wants to die. No one wants life to end. We all want to go right on living – on and on and on – forever, if we could.

But returning to the question, why are there so many religions? They all seem to come to the conclusion, 'Do Good and Reach God.' They all start out with that premise and then diverge far afield from each other in their various theories, rules, practices, and rituals. And they are all **sincere**!

Standing under the stars, grasping for an overview of the whole pattern, one is apt to conclude:

"There are probably many pathways to God, any one you choose will take you there, as long as you are sincere."

This sounds good, it sounds reasonable, but is it right? Is it correct?

One might answer, " Well, if it isn't right, then why doesn't God show us the right way? Why doesn't God reveal Himself to mankind?

Have you ever considered that perhaps He has, and you missed it?

You missed it because you have been too busy living the good life. You have been too busy with your problems and troubles. You have been too busy... to see the beauty of the sky because of all the pollution and glow around you.

Being busy, however, is not the biggest reason that people miss it. They miss it because it is totally opposed to their nature. People have a sinful nature. You say, "Hey, don't start in with that sin stuff."

Wait a minute! Most people don't even know what sin is. Ask anyone, ask yourself – what is sin? Most likely you will get answers like: adultery, cheating, lying, murder, stealing, etc. Others might answer: smoking, drinking, and doing dope.

Not surprising. But all of those are not sin. They are sins. They are only the fruit of the tree. The root structure and the trunk of the tree is sin.

So, what is sin? *It is rebelliousness toward God. Rebellion that asserts itself in Pride, Arrogance, Haughtiness, and Self-sufficiency carried to the extreme. It is the person who literally says, "I don't need God." So now we are coming down to it! On the one hand, people have a sinful nature, and on the other hand, they also have an* *instinct for immortality. Wow, what a conflict that produces!*

Three ways to resolve conflict.

First, one can run from it, try to get as far away from it as possible, by either physically distancing oneself or mentally dismissing it. Second, one can rationalize, synthesize, and compromise. And, three, one can examine it and make a choice.

Some run. One autumn afternoon, Corinne and I saddled the horses to bring in the cattle. They were in the east pasture and would have to be worked through an unfamiliar gate. When working cattle, it is best to work them slowly and casually. The worst thing that can happen is that they start to run. Lots of bad situations can develop when that breaks loose – they run off weight, they can be injured, they get excited, and so on.

As we were working them down off the hillside toward the gate, five yearling heifers separated themselves and held back. I tried to ease in behind them to encourage them to go along with the herd, but the five of them apparently decided they were going to have none of it. They jerked their heads up, lifted their tails high in the air, and took off on a dead run – in the opposite direction.

We rode hard and managed to turn them and start the process all over again. But when we reached the gate, they played the same scene all over again. And so did we. This happened four times. Now after the fourth refusal, they turned and ran toward our outside barbed-wire fences and directly through them. They ran for five miles to the foot of a giant mountain. The story becomes rather involved at this point, but the net result was two of the heifers were returned the next day, and the other three were not retrieved until the following Spring. Hyper-nervousness is a heredity trait. We don't want it. All five were shipped to slaughter.

Yes, some run. *They deny God, they deny immortality,*

they deny sinful nature, they can deny them all. But denial does not invalidate reality! A man can deny his own father, pretend he doesn't exist, completely write him off, change his name, move away, and put him completely from his mind, but...it doesn't change the fact the father exists, nor does it change the relationship.

Some compromise. When a donkey mates with a horse, the offspring is a mule. It is neither donkey or horse, it is a hybrid, — a compromise. This animal is sterile, it cannot reproduce. Therefore, one might say that for the mule there is no "after-life." Now a mule is not worthless, by any means, but the point is, its productiveness is inalterably limited to its present, physical life. Furthermore, a mule is traditionally regarded as stubborn, contrary minded having a mind of its own. A mule tends to make up its own rules.

Yes, some compromise. They attempt to synthesize their sinful nature with immortality by balancing their life so they "do good" a little more than they do bad. They make up their own rules. They independently decide if God will judge them, how He will judge them, and on what basis. They work out a neat little system they can live with. But what makes it right? And when everyone makes up his own set of rules, the rules are bound to be different, some even conflicting with others. Does this make sense? How can that possibly be right?

Some examine the evidence and make a choice. What is the choice? Either to continue to rebel, or to yield and accept.

My son and youngest daughter would select calves from our herd each year to raise and show as 4H projects. After the calf was weaned, the first thing we did was to confine them and put a halter on them. A lead rope was then fastened to the halter and the calf released. The excitement starts right then!

The calf bolts ahead on the run, only to have the lead rope snap taut, sometimes jerking him all the way to the

16

ground. The fight is on – and it takes no little amount of effort and muscle to work him into his new home. After a day or two acclimating to his new quarters, the calf is snubbed to a post. Most of them fight for awhile and then give up. Once in a while, a calf will never give up and he cannot be used.

Fireball was one of those calves who fought for days. He would stand, tied to the post, pulling against the rope for hours. He would pull so hard for so long he exhausted himself. A few times he would become so tired he fell down. It seemed like he would never give up. If he could only understand that if he would give up, he would live the good life: abundance of rich feed, special care and pampering, grooming, baths, etc. whereas his brothers out in the field were destined to the feedlot and slaughter.

His rebellion made it difficult for everyone, but primarily for himself. There he stood – four feet planted, leaning backwards, neck stretched, head at an awkward, unnatural angle, and eyeballs rolled around to show the whites – for hours on end.

Purely by coincidence (or did God plan it?) I happened to be watching him when he finally got the message. He sighed deeply and took a step forward. The tension came off, his head resumed a natural posture, his eyeballs rolled forward. I could almost see his mind working, "his wheels turning." Then he would jerk back again and pull. Then a step forward. Pull, step, pull, step. In his dull mind, he was deciding it was better for him to yield and accept than to rebel. He gave up! He was a marvelous show calf.

You have an immortality instinct. You also have a nature rebellious toward God. They are in conflict. How are you going to resolve that conflict? No one is asking you to yield and accept. All that is being asked of you is to examine the evidence and to make a choice. Just take that step forward.

CHAPTER TWO

Four Seasons

Good News!

The four seasons are wonderful! I grew up in southern California, so I was not accustomed to living with snow and ice in the wintertime. It was a surprise to me when we moved to the mountains. Of course, what is one person's delight can be another person's drudgery. Most of the world's peoples and most of the world's productiveness, however, are located in the temperate zones where there are four seasons. Each season has its redeeming qualities and beauty to offset its disadvantages. Balance. There is, indeed, balance in nature.

Summer. Many people seem to live for the summer. They feel summer is the ultimate season; the season of warmth, growth, enjoyment, vacations, and outdoor activities. Another fun thing about summer, especially in the more northerly latitudes, the days are much longer. Of course, there are climatic differences between regions that cause summertime to be wet in some areas and dry in others. However, the old show tune, "Summer time...and the living is easy..."seems universal. The world is alive and enjoying life. Plants and trees are responding by reaching toward the sky, crops progress rapidly toward maturity, and the lush grasses of the pastures fatten the cattle, sheep, and wildlife. The birds sing happily in the trees, the squirrels skitter up and down the giant trees in play. The larger animals often respond to the mating urge. And the pace of human life slackens from the hectic days of spring as people gather and relax in outdoor activities. The world is experiencing the abundance of life, the fullness of life. Summer time.

Autumn comes with the wind. With the possible exception of sailors, it is difficult to think of anyone who likes the wind. It is noisy, it is dirty, and it raises the tension level as it blows dust, dirt, leaves, pollen, trash, and anything light and loose in its path. Who could enjoy that? It bangs doors and windows, it hoots through alleyways, and it whistles through the trees and the power lines. Unsettling, to say the least. Fortunately, it doesn't blow all of the time, there are times of stillness.

But whether blowing or not, the autumn activities of harvest and storage must be completed. The crops must be gathered and loaded into the barns for the winter or sent off to processing facilities where they are sold. The fruit in the orchards must be picked and brought to the refrigerators, the processing room or the home kitchen for storage or preparation. The kitchen becomes a bee-hive of activity as the ladies cook and can tomato sauce, catsup, pickles, taco sauce, jams, jellies, sweet corn, beans, carrots, apples, peaches, pears, grapes, and others – all in their turn. The aromas floating away from the kitchen are usually strong and tell-tale. Butter and cheeses are also being made as our milk cow, Elsie, swings into production again with the arrival of her new baby calf. We deliberately breed her to freshen in the Fall.

Outside, the leaves on the trees harden and paint the

landscape with their golden, reddish strokes. The squirrels scurry everywhere in search of their winter supplies. The animals' hair and fur become thicker and heavier as nature commences to provide them with their winter overcoats. Calves are separated from their mothers and weaned, much to the noisy consternation of both bawling parties. Wood is gathered for the cold winter ahead. Pipes are wrapped and machines are brought inside. Preparations for winter proceed full steam ahead. In perspective then, the activities of autumn signify both completion and transition – concluding the summer activities of producing food and fiber; and preparations for the winter ahead. As autumn draws to a close, all the harvest is in, all preparations for the cold spell ahead are completed – it is indeed a time for **Thanksgiving**.

Winter is the season of hardship and barrenness. The wind has stripped the trees of their leaves, leaving only the ever-greens to provide a memory of the summer. Storms descend suddenly and vent their fury on the countryside. Temperatures drop drastically as winds cascade through the meadows and over the hills, pounding the rain against everything in its path. Then, almost magically, the sounds of the storm suddenly cease. No more noise. But a peek outside discloses millions of tiny snow flakes fluttering to the ground in silence. It feels rather delicious to cuddle down in your warm bed and fall off to sleep in that silence. The next morning, you arise to the most magnificent scene – the whole world is snuggly wrapped in virgin white fleece from the clouds. The world is quiet, it is still, everything seems motionless. It reminds one of death.

For those who have not made the proper preparations, winter can produce many hardships. Pipes can freeze and break – cutting off the water supply. Roads can become impassable, firewood can become soaked, animals can die from exposure, roofs can leak, structures can topple in the wind or from the weight of the snow, and life can be miserable if not, at times, almost impossible. One thing becomes patently clear – the comfort of winter depends upon the proper preparation in the autumn. Once winter arrives, it is too late.

Spring brings **'thaw.'** A funny looking four-letter word that carries such a welcome meaning. The winter ice begins to melt, the snow relaxes and morphs to muddy slush. Rivulets trickle and join hands with others to babble incoherently down the hillsides. The sun smiles down from the heavens warming the cold ground. Hope springs into the hearts of those who thought the winter would never end, those who felt they were doomed to go on and on forever in the dismal bleakness. Hope! Springtime! Good News!

The drab colors of winter magically give way to the verdant carpets of the new season. The pastures spring forth in rich, new life as the grass stretches toward the azure sky. Fruit trees burst into bloom, proudly waving their colors to all admirers. Tiny flowers blossom, blanketing the hillsides. Temperatures continue to rise to comfort levels. Animals start having their babies, trees commence leafing out in majesty – new life is evident everywhere! Finally!

Divine Design? Did God design the seasonal rotation to reflect the cycle of life? That is, in fact, a very old concept. Springtime – birth and childhood; Summer – maturity; Autumn – old age; and Winter – death. If God created the solar system, God could have arranged this planet in some other type of orbit – producing, say, continual summer time, couldn't He? But He didn't. So, are there lessons here we should be observing? Quite possibly.

Perhaps the biggest lesson is one to which we have already alluded: preparation in autumn for winter, suggesting we should be preparing for death. But what is the teaching here? Are we to wait until we are middle aged or retired before we make preparations for death? Many people do, but it is risky. Many people never make a Will, always putting it off until later – and often, later never comes.

The same is true in the spiritual realm. When reflecting about God, and death, and life after death, many people make a very curious decision. Instead of examining the evidence and making a decision, they decide "not to decide." Of course, this is a decision in itself. The result is, they never decide. And after they die, it is too late.

From city life to the ranch. We moved to the ranch in the middle of the winter. January. We were barely settled when a gigantic snow-storm hit. Pipes broke, cars and trucks were stalled and stuck, we did not have the proper clothing, we did not have a large enough supply of food for the animals, and so on. We suffered. We were not prepared. Out of our misery, I thought I learned a lesson, and vowed that next year I would be ready.

The following autumn, I bought a new four-wheel drive truck. I wrapped pipes, we bought warm, practical clothes, a large supply of hay was brought in, and all the little details were set in order. Down at the well, I turned on the light bulb next to the pump, a local practice followed to throw sufficient heat inside the enclosure to keep the pump from freezing. Anti-freeze went into all the vehicles, chains were ready. We were ready. We heralded the completion of preparation with a smugness, "let it snow, let it snow…"

It did! The first storm hit December 10th. Snow piled up over three feet deep and the temperature dropped below zero. I felt so self-confident.

The next morning, my mother (who was living with us at the time) simply said, "There is no water." No water? I ran to the faucet. It was true! I couldn't understand it, what had gone wrong? That "here-we-go-again" feeling came over me. But I dressed and climbed the hill to the holding tank, crawled up the ladder and peered in. Empty! I was confused, how could it be empty? I had just filled the big 10,000 gallon tank a few days before. I started searching, slowly and deliberately, following the 300 feet of line downward toward our home. Everything was covered with snow, but near the bottom of the hill, I found the spot where the pipe had frozen and burst – draining the tank.

Make a plan. The first thing to do, I decided, was to get the pump running and fill the tank again, holding the water in the tank while I fixed the broken pipe. A little broken pipe didn't dampen my spirits, so I hopped into the truck, dropped it into 4 wheel, and proudly plowed through the snow driving the half-mile around the hill to the well. As I stepped to the pump enclosure, I did not see anything wrong, but when I opened the hatch and peered in, I noticed the light bulb had gone out. Without its warmth, the pump had frozen and broke. We were in deep trouble!

I thought about that episode periodically, wondering if God had a lesson in it for me that I simply could not see. I had prepared myself, I could not have anticipated the light bulb burning out. Was there a lesson here? And suddenly, it all unscrambled. The light bulb is a rather universally accepted object to represent "ideas" – one's own understanding. That light bulb represented my own understanding. I had prepared myself for winter with my own understanding. It seemed reasonable, but it was insufficient.

And spiritually, we cannot prepare ourselves for death in our own understanding. It is not sufficient. The postulate we proposed in the last chapter: "Any pathway to God is sufficient as long as you are sincere," is false. I had been sincere. I had prepared according to my own understanding, but I was in exactly the same predicament I had been in when I did not prepare at all.

Do not confuse sincerity with truth. They are not the same.

The comparison of the human life to the four seasons might yield many, many lessons, but I believe God had an even greater purpose in designing the four seasons. They *exemplify God's good news. It was mentioned earlier that all the religions of the world, except one, have a common theme of "Do good and reach God." The religion that does not fit into that category is Christianity. It is completely different. Instead of that common theme mentioned, the theme of Christianity is "You are inherently bad, but God loves you." This is not mankind reaching up to God, but just the opposite, God reaching down to man. God is reaching down in love to rescue man from his dilemma. That, my friend, is really good news. Very good news! And God has written that good news right into nature! God has also written that good news more definitively in His book, the Bible.*

There is one unchangeable truth that all the sincerity in the world cannot alter. It is that <u>God is unapproachable except through Jesus.</u>

*Jesus said, **"I am the Way, and the Truth, and the Life; No one comes to the Father except through Me."** John 14:6*

Who is this Jesus? Was Jesus the Son of God as He claimed? Either He is, or He was the most self-deluded person in history, on the one hand, or the world's biggest liar on the other hand.

Lying, however, was inconsistent with His nature. There was too much kindness, too much love, too much sincerity, and no personal gain at all for Him to lie.

Self-deluded? Insane? Not reasonable. Could an insane person perform miracles of healing? Could an insane person have raised Lazarus from the dead? Could an insane person have delivered the Sermon on the Mount? Not likely. The only alternative left, then, is to take Him at His word when He said, "I am the Way..."

For years, when watching professional football games on television, one could often see persons in the stadium --I presume private citizens who have purchased tickets – who would raise up a sign that would be visible during the extra point kicks down in the end zone that would read, **John 3:16.** This Bible verse is a direct quote of Jesus saying, ***"For God so loved the world that He gave His one and only Son, that whoever believes in Him, shall not perish, but have eternal life."***

And Jesus repeatedly claimed to be God's Son. If He wasn't, how could He have done the miracles? There were 45 of them recorded before He was crucified. They were witnessed by hundreds of different people. They were never questioned as to their authenticity. They were performed for the express reason of helping people to believe that He was God's Son.

*So 'the Way' is believing in Jesus. Believing what? Believing that He actually lived, and said, and did the things attributed to Him? Yes, but if that were all, that would only be intellectual assent to the historical reality of Jesus. Is **that** the good news?*

*How about one step further? How about believing that Jesus was a good man who taught good things and that we should pattern our lives after Him? That is a nice thought, but of course, it is utterly impossible. Who can do it? Is **that** the good news – patterning our lives after Jesus?*

All right, let's go one step further yet. How about believing that Jesus is really God and He want us to be on His 'side' – against sin and evil. Perhaps the good news is that we can join forces with Jesus by living a good life, obeying His commandments, going to Church and participating, and giving money?

No, no, no, no, no! The good news is better than that! And it's simpler, too. The good news is really in two parts:

Part One: The good news is that each and every individual, you and me – the real person who lives inside our body (our soul), can become immortal, and live forever.

*Part Two: The cost for this immortality? It is **FREE!***

***Why?** Because God loves you. God loves everyone on*

the earth and wants us to be His companions for eternity... forever! God is not standing aloof in judgment and wrath, but reaching down to all mankind in love. Because God loves us so much, He wants to do unimaginable goodness for us eternally.

But for two reasons, He can't *just do it!*

First, God cannot tolerate sin. Not even the slightest little bit of it. He is perfectly holy. And mankind, each and every one of us, has a sinful nature. We were born with it. No matter how hard we try, no matter how hard we work, we cannot eliminate or eradicate our sin. It is impossible.

Second, God wants us to come to Him voluntarily. God wants our worship to stem from our own free will. He does not want to compel us to worship Him.

Dilemma. God wants us to come to Him. He wants us to be His companions, but we are sinful. It cannot be. So God provided a way. There is only ONE WAY the gulf can be spanned.

God gave His Son, Jesus Christ, to come into the world, to live a perfect sinless life and thereby be perfect and worthy. Then Jesus had to die, He had to die to act as a substitute for us. Jesus took all the sins of the world, everyone's sin – your sin and my sin –and paid the penalty for it — for me, for you.

Jesus shed His blood and died so you won't have to die. We are not talking about physical death here, but spiritual death. Not your body, but your soul –the real you, the person who lives inside your body. This idea or concept offends many people. They are repulsed by the idea of blood shedding for salvation. But the Bible, itself, cannot be more explicit. It says **"Without the shedding of blood, there is no forgiveness."** Hebrews 9:22. No forgiveness — meaning no release from the guilt or the penalty of sin.

One might think, how do I know all of this is true? Just because the Bible says this? A lot of people were executed *on a Roman cross. How do I know that Jesus paid the penalty for my sin by dying on a cross?*

This is the good part! God stamped His approval on this substitution by raising Jesus from the grave on the third day. Jesus is not dead, He is alive today and forever.

I attended the University of Arizona as an adult, a graduate student. One day I arrived at campus and had to park quite a distance from my class. As I was crossing the central grassy mall, I heard shouting and looked up to observe two groups of people facing each other, standing in a fashion like two arrowheads pointing at each other. The shouters were two young underclassmen at the point of each phalanx. One of them was blonde and fair skinned, the other had dark hair and dark skin. As I drew closer, I could hear what they were shouting. It went something like this:

Blonde: "He's dead, man"
Dark: "No, He's not. He is alive"
Blonde: "He's dead, dead, dead, two thousand years!"
Dark: "He's alive today"
Blonde: "How do you know He's alive?"
Dark: "Because He's inside me, I just know!"
Blonde: "You are crazy, He's dead, dead, dead!"

And so on it went. I continued walking to my class, but I have regretted to this day that I did not stop and silently take a place in the crowd behind the dark-skinned man as so many others were doing, sort of "voting" by their support.

What do you think? Is He alive today? Believe it and you can have eternal life, too. The concept of believing, however, is much, much more than mental assent. To believe in Jesus Christ is to put your full faith and trust into Him that He did die for your sin, personally, and that He is alive today. The price for your eternal life has already been paid for you.

My first job in the corporate world after college was as a staff aid and assistant to the Corporate Secretary of a large company in downtown Los Angeles. During my time there, they built a new building at 7th and Flower Streets, a gorgeous structure that featured floor to ceiling glass on the outside. Soon after its completion, I was called in by the Corporate Secretary and told that the productivity of the typing pool on the 12th floor had dropped to unacceptable levels. I was given the project to discover "why" and to fix it.

I have long forgotten the 'ploy' I used to go down to the 12th and hang around for awhile – to legitimize my presence down there among all those women. It did not take very long to determine what was going on. They were scared of those glass windows. They all seemed to have this secret fear they might stumble or trip, and fall against one –thus subsequently go crashing through, falling hundreds of feet to their death.

I took this information back to headquarters and it was decided to call in the architect and the building engineer to talk to the girls. The appointed day arrived, and one of the two gentlemen invited was unable to make it, so we had the meeting of everyone on the 12th floor with just the one speaker.

This man gathered everyone in the center of the room, far away from the windows, and spent a great deal of time telling them about the strength of the glass. He discussed how it was manufactured and tested, and how they could not crash through it, even if they accidentally fell against it, how inherently safe it was, and so on.

From the body language of the girls, it was evident they were being polite, but they did not believe what he was saying. After a while, our speaker just stopped. He became quiet and calm, with a resigned little smile on his face. He realized the girls did not believe him.

I have never witnessed anyone commit suicide, but I have been told, just before a person does this, they become very calm, quiet, and committed. So the thought ran through my mind as this gentlemen's shoulders slumped in resignation and he turned toward the windows. Then, without a word, he commenced running, actually sprinting, right toward the windows. As he gathered speed, it became apparent he would be unable to stop. Women screamed and shrieked and sobbed as he now approached the window at full speed. Then he jumped and spread his arms and legs out and crashed into the window!

The noise was incredible. **KABLAM!!!** I still have a sense that the building shook.

The gentleman bounced off the glass and back into the room. He had made his point. What he did was to put his "belief" into action. He put his full faith and trust into that glass to save his life.

When the Bible says "Believe on the Lord Jesus Christ and you will be saved..." it is saying to put your full faith and trust into Him. Throw yourself on Him and trust Him for your eternal safety.

What about the four seasons? *It is difficult to see God's good news in the four seasons, unless...of course, we adjust our point of view just a little bit. That's all. Instead of starting with springtime as traditionalists do, start with summer... the fullness of life. That is what Jesus was when He was on this earth., the fullness of life, perfect in every way. And he walked, and talked, and taught, and performed miracles on earth. But it did not fulfill God's plan for Jesus to continue to do this just as it was not God's plan for us to have continual summer. The autumn inevitably came. Jesus was put through terrible trials and tests, culminating in His death – winter. But the grave could not hold Him, He rose again right out of the tomb, returning to life everlasting – springtime. Yes, God wrote His good news right into nature's four seasons.*

CHAPTER THREE

Howie

The New Birth

Howie was the fruit of a program we started at the ranch after our herd bull gored me, a story related in a later chapter. I decided we didn't need real, live, flesh and blood bulls to get the job done. We realized that we could breed much better stock by artificially inseminating our herd. Consequently, I enrolled in a special school to learn how to do this, and really enjoyed the training. You know, some men love to take guns and hunt animals, kill them for sport or food – usually both – and that's fine for them. But killing non-threatening living creatures is not my thing. Helping to create them is something else.

And we do this at our ranch. We buy the seed of the finest bulls in the world, have it shipped in frozen at 320 degrees below zero, and store it in that state until the time it is needed.

Most of our cows are bred in the late spring or early summer. It takes 9 ½ months to see the results. I get excited each year as calving time approaches, even though I know the problems and troubles we sometimes encounter. And we do have our problems. But those cows seem to be worth it to me. I love each one of those bovine creatures. They each have a personality, they each have their own ways. Some are open and honest, some are cunning and crafty, some are trusting, some are suspicious, some are dainty, some are gluttonous, and the young simply jump up and down with the sheer joy of being alive.

Several years ago we selected one of our best virgin heifers to inseminate with a super European bull whose seed was flown in from Switzerland. Our little heifer conceived on the first breeding, and she grew, and she grew, and she grew until she was just short of enormous.

As her time drew near, we brought her up to a small field near the barn to watch her. This is necessary because cows frequently separate themselves from the herd and hide in the brush alone when they calve — instinctive protection against predators.

On the night of March 14th, sometime between 8:PM and 10:PM, she went into labor. Lying on the ground, she would stretch and hunch in strain, then relax, then repeat the process again. After a little bit, she would arise and turn around, sniffing the ground, like she was looking for a calf. (She had never had one, so again instinct was driving her) Shortly, she would lie down again and labor some more. Up to look, down to strain, up to look, down to strain — but nothing happened, no calf appeared.

There is no new life without a birth! *Jesus told Nicodemus, "…no one can see the kingdom of God unless he is born again." John 3:3 Eternal life is free, but there is no eternal life unless there is a new birth.*

All babies are born the same way. The first thing that happens is the water bag breaks, discharging the fluids the baby has been living in during gestation. Then the baby appears and passes through the birth canal. Shortly thereafter, the tissues in which the baby has been encased, called the after-birth, pass from the cow.

All spiritual babies are born in much the same way. The first thing that happens is an acute awareness of their rebellion toward God, producing sorrow and regret and an urgent desire to turn away from their rebellious condition. In a word, repentance. But all the sorrow and all the regret in the world will not bring new life, the baby must pass through the birth canal.

Of course, the birth canal is the cross of Jesus Christ. The baby must come forward in faith—- believing that Jesus died for his personal sin. He has to believe that Jesus paid the price for him, believe so completely that he puts his whole trust in Jesus for eternal life. He must further believe that Jesus rose from the grave and lives today, and believe that eternal life has been given to him as a result of his faith in Jesus Christ. Believing these things, man passes through the birth canal of the cross.

As after-birth naturally passes from the cow, so a natural aspect of new birth is confession. The new spiritual baby tells others, confesses his faith in Jesus Christ.

All of this is necessary, but the emphasis is on the actual birth. The emphasis is on belief. Believe with the heart. Believe with the total inner-being – the soul. Believe so deeply that your full trust and full faith is placed in Jesus Christ.

*That is the new birth. That is being saved. 'Saved' is a word that bothers some people. It has been used so much by so many people, it has all kinds of connotations. The same is true of the word 'salvation.' Saved simply means having been born again. Saved **from** eternal death, saved **for** eternal life.*

The Manner of Birth

Most cows give birth naturally, by themselves. Some

simply lie down and pop a baby. Others labor for hours in trauma and pain. Some births are beautiful, some are ugly with blood and slime, and membranes. Occasionally, a baby cannot be born naturally. He needs assistance. After a few hours of labor, it becomes apparent that the baby is not going to be born unless someone helps. The type of help needed varies from a gentle manipulation of the head to attaching chains to the ankles of the calf and pulling with every ounce of human strength available. Once in a while, it takes more than human strength, and a mechanical device like a block and tackle must be used.

By midnight, I realized the little heifer needed help. I drove up to the house and uprooted my wife, Corinne, and my son, Rick. It was not the first time they had been awakened in the middle of the night for something like this, but I always marveled at their willingness and good attitude.

Armed with our obstetrical chains, we approached the cow about thirty minutes after midnight. Corinne held the flashlight, Rick moved in to manipulate the head, while I hooked the chains over the ankles and pulled. I pulled and pulled, with every ounce of strength I could muster. Soon I just gave way in exhaustion, while Rick took over the pulling as I lay on the ground hyper-ventilating. Shortly Rick started huffing and puffing, so we switched again. This time, I hooked the chains in my arms at the elbows and grabbed the collar of my coat with my hands. While Rick gently manipulated the head, I leaned my entire body weight against the resistance, rocking forward and back. Finally......

Kazowie! There's Howie! Was he born quickly! He came so fast that I did a backward somersault, entangling myself in the chains and the goo and slime. And Howie did all the right things – he shook his head, blinked his eyes, and started breathing deeply. He was born alive!

Not all babies experience the same kind of birth.

Although they are all born the same way, their birth experience is not the same. Everyone who is born again must pass through the narrow birth canal and come to Jesus Christ through the cross of calvary. They must ask Jesus to forgive their sin, they must invite Jesus to come into their heart. They must believe.

But the manner in which they are born can be varied. Many narrow-minded Christians fail to see this. Some people simply hear the good news and believe, just like the cow that lies down and pops a baby. Others have a long, traumatic birth with tears and violent sobs wracking the body. Some need help. There are many different manners in which people can pass through the same birth canal, the cross of Jesus Christ.

The Baby's Reaction

Regardless of how the little baby calves are born, the babies themselves all react differently upon their birth. Some jump right up to their feet with the natal sack and placenta still hanging all over them, and start bawling to be fed. Most of them, however, simply shake their heads, blink their eyes a few times and lie there quietly. Sometimes a new-born will lie perfectly still with its eyes shut and one has to look very carefully to see if it is breathing.

*It's the same way with new Christians. Some start shouting and jumping up and down with joy. Others sit quietly and weep. Still others become frozen and immobile in the awe of the Lord. Some don't **feel** anything, but they **know** in their hearts, the Holy Spirit has confirmed their salvation.*

I read an article a while back that stated the opinion that the New Birth has been over-sold. As I sat thinking about it, I realized some truth in it. Too many searching souls are led to believe – either by someone's testimony or by inference – that if they accept Jesus Christ as their personal savior, He'll change their life so completely that

they will be perfect. *And so, they take the step of faith, and soon realize that they have not become perfect. This is when they find out they have not been 'transformed' into perfect. Often, they become discouraged, some even give up. The new birth doesn't make one perfect on earth. It makes one perfect in the eyes of God. It means one has accepted Jesus Christ, His Son, in his heart – personally – and has put his full faith, trust, and life in Jesus hands. Under these conditions, Jesus guarantees eternal life. He said so.*

Most brand new Christians experience joy – abounding, unspeakable, unimaginable joy – when they are born again. A tremendous load seems to have been lifted from their souls. They experience a deep, inward peace, a sense of boundless freedom, and love permeates their soul. Joy, freedom, peace, and love....all are associated with the new birth.

Naming the Babies

On the ranch, before our calves are born, each of them receives an individual number – his name, if you will. If that particular calf lives, that number is put in his ear. If he does not live, that number is never used again, for it was designed for that specific individual. The way our system works that number is lost forever.

The Bible says when a person is born again, his name is written in the Book of Life. Have you ever wondered what your name is in heaven? Or even if it is there? Obviously, it cannot be your present name, there are just too many duplications. Yet, whatever your name is in heaven, it inspires JOY to know that it is there. What emotion, except pure joy, could have inspired C. Austin Miles to write the old gospel song, "There's a new name written down in glory, and it's mine, oh yes, it's mine...?"

Out in the pasture, when we see evidence of new life, we rejoice! We are happy, we are glad, we are exhilarated. The same thing happens when a new baby is born into the kingdom of God. The Bible says **"...there is rejoicing in the presence of the angels of God over one sinner who repents."** Luke 15:10

A number of years ago, a woman vocalist, who has been entertaining for years with dance bands and also in Las Vegas, came out with a rather melancholy song entitled, " Is that all there is?" If you ever hear it, listen to the words. They are a commentary on a seemingly full and rich life, yet asking the question, "Is that all there is?" It implies that there must be something more. It describes a full life that is still empty, there is something lacking, there is no real satisfaction. Is that all there is?

Of course, the answer to her is, and to all others who might think along the same lines, "No, there is one thing you missed, **the new birth."**

CHAPTER FOUR

Gored!

Satan Attacks!

One day, many summers ago, we rounded up the cattle herd to perform a little work on them. The purpose of that little round-up has long since been forgotten, but it was probably to treat the animals to ease their suffering from flies and warbles during the summer.

At that time, we still had a herd bull, a large, registered horned Hereford. That bull had been on the ranch for three years. On two occasions prior to this incident, this bull had shown signs of aggression. He should have been shipped.

All the animals, the bull, the cows and all the little calves were gathered in the corral. I stepped into the corral and started sorting cattle. I knew where the bull was – over in the far corner just standing placidly. Absentmindedly, I turned away from him to push some calves through a gate, waving my arms and making a little noise.

The next thing I knew, I had been hit squarely – an absolute 'bulls-eye' – right in the middle of the rump by this incredibly powerful force. I was lifted up off the ground and catapulted through the air in an upright swan dive form. I arced through the air, and then hit the ground. I was stunned. It all happened so suddenly. Before I could recover, the bull had his head right down next to mine and I could feel his hot breath on my neck. Then I felt the most terrible pain I have ever felt in my life under my left arm. I thought he was stepping on me. The bull snorted and pushed against me, and I felt my body being lifted off the ground and tossed toward the fence. In a flash, I realized the bull was working me over to the fence where he intended to pound the life out of me. I started to yell!

My brother, Steve, who was also in the corral, reacted the quickest. He grabbed the bull by the tail, pounded him with a stick, shouting at him. The bull was distracted, and I was able to roll under the fence and get out of the corral. I got to my feet on the other side of the fence and immediately went into shock. Shock is a strange thing, it does different things to different people. It affected me that day in two ways: nausea and fever – both almost instantly. I felt sick to my stomach, but didn't throw up; and I could not get enough cold water.

My brother and his friend, Jim, took me up to the house where I laid down on the yard table. I remember complaining about where the bull had stepped on me. They took a look at it, and quickly realized I had not been stepped on, but gored, and blood was spurting. Both of these men were recent Army combat veterans and they realized the bleeding could be internal and that I should be transported to the hospital as fast as possible.

It was an hour's drive from the ranch into town and the hospital. During the entire bumpy trip, Jim held two fingers in the wound. I kept telling him the two fingers in there hurt me more than the wound did, but he refused to take them out.

They were waiting for us when we drove up to the hospital because Rick had called to alert them concerning my injury. I was helped onto a gurney quickly and whisked into the emergency room. The doctor on duty spent a long time in the examination. I was made to lift my left arm several times, make a fist, cough, etc. He said the bull's horn had entered twice – both times into my torso, right where the arm joins the body, in the rear. One plunge had gone about six inches into the thoracic cavity, and the other had only gone two or three inches up into the arm, near the shoulder area. The doctor felt I was indeed fortunate to have two horn punctures that missed the lung and the heart, missed all the major arteries and veins, and missed all the important motor and sensory nerves. In addition, had the bull not hit me so squarely in the first place, I would have had a broken back and possibly permanent paralysis.

The wounds were classified as deep flesh wounds. I was treated, medicated, and dressed with a couple of drainage tubes inserted deep in me, then released.

I did not heal 100%. Even today, years later, I cannot raise my left arm over my head without pain. And an area about the size of a silver dollar where the puncture was made, has had absolutely no feeling in it ever since. Scar tissue.

Satan will attack you when you least expect it!

New Christians, newly born babes in Christ, are special targets. One of Satan's favorite weapons is doubt. As doubt is implanted in their minds, new Christians become confused. They start to wonder if they **really were** born again. Satan whispers, "How can you be born again? You didn't act or react in such and such a manner." Or, on the other hand, if the new Christian had a violent, shaking birth with painful repentance and groaning of the spirit, Satan might taunt them, "You were not **really** born again, you just let yourself get caught up in an emotionally charged atmosphere. You just let your own emotions get *away from you."*

Satan tries to divert the new Christian's attention away from the **fact** of the new birth, and from **faith** in Christ, by throwing doubts in the area of **feelings** and **experience**. When this happens, and it most surely will, remember that Jesus said, **"...whoever believes in Him shall not perish, but have everlasting life."** *John 3:16b*

This statement encompasses both fact and faith, but does not mention anything about feeling.

Anytime that a living soul places faith in Jesus Christ and is born again, you can be sure there is one who **does not** rejoice. Satan. He is infuriated. He hates to lose anyone, but he can't do anything about it. He cannot rob you of your salvation, so he does the next best thing. He tries to defuse the new babe in doubt and confusion.

<u>**Satan will attack on the heels of any Spiritual victory.**</u> You can count on it. These times will be

- Anytime God answers prayer and Christians rejoice.
- Anytime God undertakes to solve seemingly unsolvable problems.
- Anytime God heals bodies, or souls, or hearts.
- Anytime God provides when there is no other provision.
- Anytime Christians are rejoicing in a spiritual glow.

Walk carefully............Satan will probably attack. He will do his best to rob you of the victory, he will do his best to steal the glow. Be alert!

<u>**Satan will attack you in a way in which you are MOST vulnerable!**</u>

I always shudder when I hear ministers taunt Satan from

the pulpit. I have heard them arrogantly challenge Satan to even try to strike a blow. I have heard them say something to the effect of, " Satan is already defeated. He is a loser. He cannot destroy those who are in Christ. Get thee behind me, Satan, and be gone."

Well, it is true. Satan is already defeated in God's great plan. Jesus broke Satan's bondage of death. Satan has lost, Satan cannot destroy a Christian's soul, because Jesus lives there and because Jesus guarantees eternal life.

But, Satan is still the prince of this world. Check John 12:31. Satan is powerful, intelligent, clever, and cunning. No man in the flesh is a match for Satan. Jesus told us to fear him – not taunt him. This is what Jesus said about it,

"Do not be afraid of those who kill the body, but cannot kill the soul. Rather be afraid of the One who is able to destroy both soul and body in hell." Matthew 10:28

Notice the change in case from '*those who…*' to '*the One who…*' This passage obviously refers to the second death, but don't be deceived – Satan is able to destroy on this earth – now. If this is not true, then explain the plight of the Christians of the early church being fed to the lions in the Coliseum in Rome. Explain the Christian martyrs who died at a burning stake. Explain present day missionaries who are murdered by uncivilized savages.

Most of the time, however, Satan prefers to destroy more subtly. He tries to discredit Christ by discrediting Christians. He knows the weakest, most vulnerable spots in which to attack. Christians, especially Christians who are not well plugged in to their power source, go waltzing along merrily on their way, only to be tripped. And they fall…their testimony is discredited, invalidated, and damaged. Satan is in glee – he has won the first round, and

Fireflies

he moves in for the second.

The Christian goes into shock. " How could God let that happen?" – and reacts in sorrow and humiliation. From there, Satan doesn't have to push too hard to shove him over the brink into discouragement and despair. Indeed, even depression can result. This victory is gone. Defeat is too humiliating. The wounds might heal, but the scars remain as a reminder.

On the ranch we occasionally encounter a rattlesnake. When they were young, my children and grandchildren were taught to leave the snake alone and to come to us and tell us where it was so we could dispatch it. They were carefully instructed to never, never, never "play" with the snake. Never to pick up sticks and tease it or taunt it, not to throw stones at it, not to even disturb it. By the same token, the children were warned not to go searching for a snake, they might find one.

The Bible tells us we can do one of two things when encountering Satan. First, we can resist him. Here is what the Bible says about it.

> *"Resist the devil, and he will flee from you."*
> *James 4:7b*
>
> *"Be self-controlled and alert; Your enemy, the devil prowls around like a roaring lion looking for someone to devour. Resist him, standing firm in the faith..." I Peter 5:8-9*

But there is a condition, and it is found in Ephesians 6:11 **" Put on the full armor of God so that you can take your stand against the devil's schemes."** It is not wise to try to resist Satan without the whole armor of God!

Second, if we are not protected with the whole armor of God, it is Biblical to run from temptation. The books of First

Corinthians and First Timothy contain references to this.

Bottom line: ***Stay in constant contact with the One who issues the armor.***

CHAPTER FIVE

Boysenberries

The True Vine

We selected our home site in the autumn, and before any of the building was started, we planted our family orchard. From as long as I could remember, I had had a desire for a gigantic berry patch. Consequently, one of the first things we did was to lay out a patch and buy two dozen boysenberry plants. Bare root. And that is about all there was, just a little clump of roots.

Each clump was buried in its appointed spot. Early in the spring, shoots could be observed penetrating the surface. They grew like wild fire. Trellises were erected to control the direction of their growth. The shoots quickly became long branches that were woven in and out of the trellises.

Berries are interesting. The vines are extremely thorny. Each year fruit bears on last year's growth. Our berries are the first fruits to ripen in the year – our first harvest. After the berries are picked, the branches that bore the fruit are completely cut off to the ground. They are no longer necessary, in fact, they must be cut off to avoid the berry patch from becoming a terrible mess of entangled brambles. During the summer, new growth appears which grows from five to fifteen feet long. These branches are woven into the trellis as they will bear the following spring. Occasionally, when we are weaving the branches through the trellis wires, a branch will kink. The kink cuts off the trailing end of the branch from the root structure and the branch eventually dies.

Jesus said, "I am the true vine, and my Father is the gardener. He cuts off every branch in me that bears no fruit, while every branch that does bear fruit, He prunes so it will be even more fruitful. John 15:1-2 The comparison is interesting.

Each clump was buried – *as Christ was buried after He died for our sins on Calvary.*

Each clump sent forth shoots, rising from its earthly grave—*as Christ came out of the grave and is our living Lord.*

Each vine sends out branches, — *and Jesus said we are the branches.*

The branches are thorny – *and we Christians are not perfect either, just attached to the vine.*

Each season the branches that have born fruit are removed. This fact can have perhaps three applications – (1) branches are purged to bring forth more fruit; (2) each individual must continue to grow year by year in order to keep producing fruit; or (3) each generation gives way to the next in the cause of Christ.

*If there is anything that is vitally important to Christians in their daily living, in their Christian walk, it is Jesus' words, "**Remain in Me**..." John 15:4 The branch must be in constant contact with the root source. The Christian must be in constant contact with Christ through prayer. There can be no fruit without it.*

Many new Christians don't really know how to pray. The disciples had the same problem, so they asked Jesus to *teach them how to pray. He gave them an example – a prayer pattern to follow. Because so many folks are familiar and comfortable with this prayer as it is rendered in the 1611 Authorized Version, it will be used here:*

> **Our Father which art in heaven, Hallowed be Thy Name**
> **Thy Kingdom come, thy will be done, in earth as it is in heaven.**
> **Give us this day our daily bread.**
> **And forgive us our debts, as we forgive our debtors;**
> **And lead us not into temptation, but deliver us from evil**
> **For thine is the kingdom and the power, and the glory, forever. Amen.**

Translation. The prayer above is the generally accepted version from the King James, but is not exactly the same in various King James Bibles. It is also not exact between Matthew 6:9-13 and Luke 11:2-4.

Old English Let me say one thing before we start our commentary on this prayer. The King James Version or translation of the Bible was made almost 400 years ago. Our language has changed immensely since then. The KJV uses archaic words, archaic phrases, and quite often is misleading.

But frankly, there seems to be a vast number of people who believe that this is *some kind of holy language that must be adhered to when speaking to God*. I have listened to people who talk normally in twenty first century English all the time, but the minute they start to say a public prayer, they shift into "thee, thy, thou, sayest, didst, shouldest, etc. *I really wonder what is going through their minds.* Consider this fact: The original New Testament was written in the **common** Greek language of the day, not the classical Greek of 400 years earlier. Ponder on this fact, I believe it is important. We will discuss this more in a later chapter. Nevertheless, the example follows.

Our Father, which art in heaven, Hallowed be thy name.
The prayer pattern starts with recognition of God as our Father. He is the source of our life. We honor Him, we are polite and courteous, we are reverent and respectful, we say, " Our Father" not "Hey, Dad!" Yet at the same time, we can call Him Father – there is no need to become involved in long, pompous introductions. Have you ever heard something like, " Almighty God, Eternal Creator of the Universe and Magnificent Giver of Life to all thy people, and all good things. . .?" Jesus did not use that type of introduction and He did not instruct us to do so. Just "Father."

Our Father encompasses so much. ' Dear God, you are my Father, I recognize you as my God in heaven. Everything about you is holy, even your name is holy, and I bow before you right now – recognizing and admitting your holiness, and worshipping you for it. You are first, Father, you come first in heaven above, you come first on earth below. You are the source of life – I glorify you first and foremost.'

"Thy kingdom come, Thy will be done, in earth, as it is in heaven."
'Lord, it is so easy and natural for me to request things from you that are MY will, but it is Your Will which is really important. You are the all-knowing One, You are the all-seeing One, You are the all understanding One. You know the past, you know the present circumstances, you know what the future holds. Lord, I pray that Your Will be accomplished here on earth. I pray that Your Will be accomplished in my life. Give me the sensitivity and the wisdom and the submissiveness to recognize Your Will. Reveal Your Will, O Lord, that I may glorify You in obedience and love.'

"Give us this day our daily bread."
'Father, you have sustained me since birth. Please continue to provide for my needs as you have in the past. I recognize I need daily sustenance in my spiritual life and ask you to guide me in my daily Bible reading. Open my spiritual eyes so Your Word will feed me and nourish me and produce growth.

And Father, I pray for my physical needs for this day alone. Not for riches, not for success, not for fame, but just my needs for today. Help me to trust in you completely, a day at a time. You know my problems, You know my pain, You know my troubles, You know my weaknesses, You know my desires. Lord, I just turn all of these over to You and simply ask for You to provide for me today.'

"Forgive us our debts as we forgive our debtors,"
Over the four centuries since the King James translation, these words 'debts' have morphed through 'trespasses' to 'sins.'

'Lord, I know you have already forgiven me for my sins, and all you want is for me to confess that I have sinned. I am sorry, Lord, really sorry that I fall so short of your holiness and righteousness. Thank you for loving me so much that You have forgiven my sins. I have no intention of accepting your daily sustenance in order to keep on sinning, but I do sin. Thank you for Your forgiveness.'

'And help me to forgive those who sin against me, just as Jesus forgave those who sinned against Him. Melt my heart with love and tenderness, lift me above the hurt and pain, heal my injury with Your Spirit, so I can forgive others...as You have helped me to do in the past. Lord, show Your love and reveal Yourself to those who sin against me. Be gentle and kind with them. I pray for their souls, that they might find Jesus Christ as their personal Savior and make Him the Lord of their life.'

And lead us not into temptation, but deliver us from Evil,
 'Help me to walk with You, Lord, so I might not stray into temptation. I am just a weak person and realize that in my own strength, I am no match against Satan's power. Rescue me, Jesus, when I come under Satan's attack. Provide an escape for me, Lord, so I might not sin against You.'

For thine is the Kingdom, and the Power, and the Glory, forever. Amen.

> *Yours, O Lord, is the greatness and the power and the glory, and the majesty and the splendor, for everything in the heaven and the earth is yours. Yours, O Lord, is the kingdom; you are exalted as head over all. Wealth and honor come from you, You are the ruler over all things. In Your hands are strength and power to exalt and give strength to all. Now, our God, we give you thanks, and praise your glorious name.'*
>   ***I Chronicles 29:11-13***

The pattern is clear enough:
- Put God first and praise Him
- Pray for and submit to God's Will
- Petition for your needs (not wants) both spiritual and temporal
- Forgiveness, especially for you to forgive others
- Pray for His help in your daily walk
- Praise and worship Him.

Remain in Jesus. Constant, daily contact with the source of power can only be kept with prayer!

CHAPTER SIX

Living Water

Bible Study

Several natural springs can be found on our ranch. At various locations, water has found its way to the surface. In some cases it perks out; in others, it only seeps. One of those areas was developed for a shallow well. A large cavern, about 12 feet by 12 feet, was dug out fifteen feet deep and cemented. At the bottom was bed-rock, and out of the bed-rock bubbled a spring of sweet, fresh water. The spring fills the cavern, and a pump added to the structure pumps the water into a large holding tank on the top of the hill. That was our water system.

There are three big advantages of spring water on our ranch. First, it is easy to get at no great expense. Second, it is no difficult task to obtain the water, and the third advantage is that the water is sweet. It has a good, satisfying taste. There are no strong mineral or chemical tastes.

But there are disadvantages, also. One of them is that the springs occasionally dry up. When they do, we don't know how long it might be until they start flowing again. Another disadvantage is the possibility of contamination. We have not been troubled with this, but the possibility is there. Our State refused to certify this shallow well because of this reason. But the water is clean and delicious.

Shallow water

Shallow water is sweet water, living water, easy to get, yet unreliable. Contamination is always a possibility.

The thought struck me how much the shallow springs are like indiscriminate Bible reading. Many Christians cruise through the Word, searching for sweet water and quick refreshment. It is satisfying for the moment, yet is not sufficient to carry one through the drought periods. While it quenches the thirst, it is not abundant enough to provide a Christian reliably through the trials, troubles, and problems of life.

Many Christians pick up their Bible one day and read a bit from the Psalms, discovering praise or promises that enrich them. The next day, they might explore an Epistle, finding a nugget of God's treasure in the stream bed. But, by and large, they are missing the great lessons of the Bible, they are missing the important teachings of the Bible. They are missing the abundant water that will carry them through the drought, the hard times.

Deep Water

Prior to building our home, it was necessary to drill another well. This was a new adventure, and not without a degree of risk! Excitement abounded as the well-driller's heavy truck backed into place and set up for the operation. Without ceremony, or any dramatics, the driller commenced. The giant drill turned slowly into the earth, expelling soil back up as it went down. The drill went through the top-soil quickly and then slowed as it hit the first layer of rock. Time passed. Down, down, down went the drill. Section after

Fireflies

section was methodically added to the drilling pipe. Past rock layers, through gravel layers, back into rock layers, so it went. At one hundred feet, no water. Down, down continued the bit. One hundred fifty feet, no water. The final and ultimate determination concerning how deep to go is left to the man paying the bill. It is an economic decision.

In that respect, it was already hurting, but the nod was given to continue. At one hundred eighty feet, the driller stopped to examine the soil. It looked like nothing but dry powder, bone dry, but he seemed to feel from experience that this particular stratum indicated water was near. It was difficult to believe, looking at that barren dust, but he was allowed to continue. Ten more feet, no change. Five more feet and **KAWOOSH!!!!** A gusher of water exploded to the surface. Up from the depths came living water, flowing copiously! A pump was quickly put on the well and a determination was made that there was sufficient water, indeed, abundant water. The well was a good one.

The water was tasted and tested. It was not sweet, it was strong. The test showed large mineral contents in the water, primarily iron.

Drilling through topsoil, drilling through bed-rock, drilling through dry sand and gravel . . . digging, digging, digging. Hard work and costly, but eventually it produced an abundance of water, water sufficient for all our needs. Not sweet water, but strong water, full of iron.

Isn't this a picture of Bible study? Bible study that is consistent, that is costly in terms of time, that digs straight down through the layers of dry material and inevitably produces an abundance of rich, living water. Strength is added to the Christian when he partakes of this water due to the ever-present spiritual minerals. The supply is abundant and reliable, it will carry through the longest trials.

To carry the analogy one step further, the deep well is carefully sealed with concrete and steel so no contaminants can enter. The shallow well can be contaminated from the surface, the deep well cannot.

There are people in this world who are willing to contaminate God's Word. There are people who change or pervert the spirit of God's Word. There are people who preach 'another Jesus' (II Corinthians 11:4), people who teach salvation by good works, people who add legalistic elements to the gospel, people who take away the deity of Jesus, who preach some other Way than the Cross. Prolonged contact with these people could lead the shallow-water Christian into error. The deep-water Christian cannot be contaminated because the Word is sufficient and exposes the errors for what they are.

On a larger scale, people who depend on shallow water become nomads, roaming from place to place in search of water. What they find certainly keeps them alive, but they are constantly on the move toward the next oasis.

On the other hand, consider modern agriculture. Many farms are sinking deep wells and investing in expensive, sophisticated irrigation equipment. The deep wells are bringing up such an abundance of water, it can be distributed to previously dry, barren ground, that in turn brings forth crops to feed the world.

The picture seems clear now. **Shallow water Christians** *are constantly on the move, searching for a new experience. But experience will not maintain them. They must constantly be on the move – from one church to another, from one fellowship to another, from one personality to another. Although they are alive spiritually, they do not have the resources or equipment to spread the Living Water.*

Deep water Christians *must remain close to their water source. They must stay close to their "investments"— their deep wells. But those wells, the results of foundational Bible studies and organizations that promote them, spread the Living Water to the previously dry and barren world. Fruit* *comes forth. Crops are harvested for Jesus Christ.*

If you are a "casual" Bible reader, why don't you consider investing some of your time in methodical, consistent Bible study? If a study group is not available, many of the Christian colleges and Bible schools have correspondence programs. Write to them.

CHAPTER SEVEN

Dividend

God's Ways

Corinne wanted a sheep. She had learned to spin, had received a spinning wheel for her birthday, and found spinning and weaving a delightful and rewarding pastime. Now she wanted a sheep. More wool.

She made a few calls around, and eventually located a Karakul ewe that was for sale. She made the deal right there on the telephone, sight unseen. In addition, or rather as part of the deal, my wife was clever enough to specify that the ewe be bred. The seller agreed, but it was to be thirty days or more before we could pick up the sheep to bring her home.

The appointed time finally arrived and we fixed up a pen in the back of our pickup truck and drove the 23 miles down to the ranch where Corinne's new sheep was waiting. Corinne had decided to call her ewe "Annie."

Catching Annie, who was among the flock, was no little task, but eventually she was separated, roped, and loaded into the truck. Then there was a little discussion about perhaps buying another sheep to keep her company because sheep tend to get so lonesome. The seller agreed and then suggested she would just give us another ewe, one who was sterile. We accepted the sterile ewe, who was named "Taja," and loaded her in with Annie and took off for home.

The autumn was uneventful. The ewes seemed happy in their new quarters and were a welcome addition to our barn.

One January afternoon, as I was working in my office in the barn, I heard a strange little sound from the ewe's stall. Upon investigation, I found a beautiful brown lamb with Annie in attendance. I removed the lamb and Annie to a specifically prepared lambing stall and left them to be together. Then after a while, another precious tiny brown lamb appeared. Twins!

Amid fragile little bleatings, the lambs appeared to have found their breakfast, and Annie, although somewhat nervous and jittery, seemed to have accepted them as well. But, as you probably know, *things are not always as they appear to be.*

Now, lambing was a first for both Corinne and me, and Annie too for that matter. We had had older lambs before, purchased and fattened, but never had a ewe give birth at our place. We didn't realize that it is not uncommon for lambs to be refused milk from their mother, especially if the mother is a first-timer.

Both lambs were healthy and eager for about a day and a half, but then they started going downhill. We started asking around concerning what could be wrong, but received unsatisfactory answers. About that time, the first lamb died. I removed the dead lamb from the stall, and Annie seemed terribly concerned; bleating, and nuzzling the other lamb. But, what we didn't know was that she was not allowing the lamb to feed.

Corinne and I checked on them in the late evening. Corinne was particularly upset and concerned. Parenthetically, Corinne was a new Christian. Upon accepting Jesus Christ as her personal Savior, one of her first resolutions was to read the Bible through completely from cover to cover, beginning to end.

She did it, too. She particularly remembered one passage in the Sermon on the Mount where Jesus said, **"Ask, and it shall be given to you…"** Matthew 7:7a

So Corinne bowed her head right there in the stall, and prayed for the safety and health of the remaining little lamb. She loves to call animals and birds, "God's little creatures." When she had finished praying, she looked up at me and said, "Everything will be alright." Her faith radiated from her face, she believed God would answer her prayer.

The second lamb was dead the next morning. I removed it from the stall when I went down early to feed the animals, and told Corinne about it when I returned for breakfast. Corinne was devastated! Her faith was totally shattered! She could not understand why God did not answer her prayer and honor her faith. This seemingly insignificant loss (compared to the bigger and more important things of life) produced a real trial in her life. Didn't Jesus say, **"Ask, and it shall be given unto you…?"** Why, God, why? Annie had given birth to two perfect little lambs and now they were both dead.

Annie was put back in the stall with Taja, and we accepted the fact that we were not going to have lambs this year. Nevertheless, we were still concerned about the loss. One day, about a week later, I saw an article in a farm magazine about many new lambs starving to death. As I read it, I realized that was what happened to our lambs. Poor things! Their mother had not let them feed! Oh, if we could only start over again! We both resolved it would be different next year.

Another couple of weeks passed without incident. One evening as I was studying in my office in the barn, I heard a strange noise coming to me. I must have heard it two or three times before it registered on my consciousness. It sounded like a new lamb. Impossible! Annie had given birth, and Taja was sterile. But what was this sound? I went out to investigate. The sound was coming from the sheep's stall, all right. I tiptoed over to look.

Taja had become a mother!

We left Taja and her new baby alone for about three hours and then decided we had better do our part in saving this lamb. We entered the stall, I wrestled Taja to the ground and held her, while Corinne held the tiny new lamb up for his breakfast. He ate ravenously! We repeated this process the next morning, and that was all it took. Taja, from that time on, accepted her lamb. The lamb grew and prospered.

We reflected on what the lesson or lessons were gathered from this episode. Was the lesson that if a new-born babe is not fed, it will die? I hardly think so. This is a truth, but not a lesson. The babies were not fed because of Annie's fear and timidity, and because of our ignorance. In the spiritual realm, Jesus is the shepherd. He knows what to do. He knows how to feed his newborn babes.

Perhaps one of the lessons is that God will not 'excuse' us for not doing our part. God will not excuse our ignorance, will not excuse our laziness, or our presumptuousness. In other words, God will not do for us what we could have done or should have done for ourselves. This concept has been challenged by some preachers who claim it is anti-Biblical. Frankly, I don't understand this charge. The Bible seems to teach it.

Let's get one thing straight. There is no way a person can accomplish his own salvation. No way. A person must totally, completely, and fully trust in Jesus Christ for salvation. But that is not the issue here.

We cannot violate God's natural laws through willful, ignorant, or good-intended actions, inactions, or neglect, and then expect God to miraculously undertake for us. As a general rule, He will not. Undoubtedly there are exceptions to this in unusual circumstances. And why should He? God works miracles to glorify His Son, Jesus Christ, so that people might believe in Him.

If we want to raise corn, but mistakenly plant milo seed, we are going to get milo. If we plant nothing at all, we cannot expect anything to come up, grow, and make a crop for us. If we feed poison to our animals, they are going to die. Surely, God can intervene in any of these circumstances, if He has a purpose and a Will to do so, but only to glorify His Son – not to bail us out of our ignorance or neglect.

But I believe God **does help** those who help themselves by stepping forward in faith. The key here is not just stepping forward, but stepping forward in faith. That is, fully doing our part, and all the while trusting in God to accomplish that which is greater and stronger than our abilities, intelligence, or understanding.

Goliath is a excellent example of this principle. God did not dispatch Goliath until someone stepped up and offered to meet him in combat. God could have disposed of Goliath in a number of ways. He could have struck him blind. He could have stricken him with a heart attack, He could have given him a disease or sickness. But God did not! Someone had to step forward in faith. David did his part. David went forward into battle, believing God would undertake the victory. David hurled the stone – I'm sure with all his might and with the full force and power of his young arms. God guided the stone directly to the vulnerable part!

The baby lamb had not eaten in the first three hours of life. The ewe was a first timer, shy and timid. No matter how much prayer we might have sent up for this lamb, it would have been 'wrong' prayer, i.e. praying for God to use His supernatural power to accomplish something that we could actually do for ourselves – hold the lamb up for his true breakfast.

*But the biggest lesson we derived from this incident is that God does honor the faith of His believers, but in **His** way. In our walk through life, we should constantly remember that God's ways are not always immediately understood or revealed to us. Sometimes we can't understand why God has allowed something to happen, or has not answered an honest, sincere prayer offered in faith. We feel like God has let us down. Yet, we are trying to understand God's ways with our own finite comprehension. Corinne was a rather new Christian when this event happened. Perhaps the lesson was we are to trust Him in faith and accept whatever happens concerning the manner in which He chooses to answer prayers.*

We named the new lamb, " Dividend."

CHAPTER EIGHT

Elsie

Worship

Elsie is our milk cow. What a delight she has been to our family! Nowhere do we get so much for so little. We feed her a little grain and hay each day, and brush her, pet her, talk to her, provide water for her, and generally minister to her needs as required. In turn, she produces a beautiful little calf each year, three to five gallons of milk each day, and an abundance of manure. All of it is utilized. The calf becomes veal for the family. The milk supports our chickens and our pigs, the cats and our dog, in addition to providing all the milk our family needs for the table. The milk also is processed into butter and cheese, and is used for cooking. As she must be milked twice a day, we have regulated our life-style to accommodate this routine activity.

If you are around a cow for any length of time, you will soon notice that a cow likes to do the same thing, at the same time, in the same place, in the same way.

Now a cow can be compared to Christ. A cow gives birth and provides food for her baby. *Christ gives the New*

Birth and provides food for His babies. A cow provides such an abundance of food that there is plenty for all – yet she gives it but a squirt at a time. *Christ has provided an overwhelming abundance of food in the Bible, there is plenty for all – yet it can only be given and absorbed little by little.*

And as for a cow being a creature of habit, the Bible says, **"Jesus Christ is the same yesterday and today and forever."** Hebrews 13:8

But these are not the lessons God showed me about cows. A cow becomes very accustomed to doing the same thing, at the same time, in the same place, in the same way. The truth is, she likes it this way! Upset her routine and observe what happens. She becomes restless, confused, perhaps even cross. She will tell you by her actions, her voice, and she might even hold back some of her milk. Yes, she can do that.

It dawned on me that many Christians and church-goers have become, *not* like Jesus, but like cows. Their desire for 'comfort' has led them into a sameness in worship. They go to the same church, at the same time, and sit in the same place, week after week. Hey – there is nothing wrong with that. In fact, it is a desirable characteristic. Loyalty, support. But it doesn't end there. Inside, week after week after week after week, it is usually the same! They call it the worship service.

Corinne and I were invited by another couple to attend their church with them on Sunday morning. Their church is a major denominational, typical cathedral-type edifice in the center of town. As we approached the church, the chimes rang from the campanile with their vibrant call to worship. Beautifully dressed people by the dozens converged upon the giant doors at the top of the steps.

Once inside the narthex, we were welcomed by an usher, given a bulletin, and taken to an empty pew in the

Fireflies

sanctuary. A glance around the building revealed the church was almost full, perhaps five hundred people or more. The heavy beamed ceiling towered high over the congregation while the stained glass windows sparkled near the top of the lofty walls. A majestic pipe organ alternately thundered and wailed through a lengthy prelude to worship.

Our bulletin listed an order for the service, the first item being "# 193 in our hymnals — Congregation please rise." At the appointed time, the heavily-robed Pastor stepped to the pulpit as the organ concluded the introduction, and the congregation rose almost in unison and sang # 193. The Pastor then read the Morning Scripture Reading (item #2 in the bulletin) which was John 4: 5-24…the concluding verse of which is…

God is spirit: and his worshipers must worship in spirit and in truth."

The Pastor then read a prayer (item #3 in the bulletin – Pastoral Prayer). After everyone was re-seated, the pastor proceeded to welcome every one to the Sunday Morning Worship Service (item #4 in the bulletin – welcome) concluding with a request to turn to # 78 in the Hymnals and join him –(item 5 in the bulletin). After the song, we listened to the announcements of church activities and socials (item #6). Out of nowhere, the ushers appeared with the offering plates (item 7) and commenced passing them up and down the pews. At the appropriate time, the organ struck a responsive chord, and everyone in the church stood up again and commenced singing the Doxology (item #8), while the ushers brought the bulging offering plates to the altar.

We were then favored with a soprano solo. The title of that song I have long forgotten because I became so engrossed in watching the Pastor talk with the Assistant Pastor – turning in their seats and holding their hands to the sides of their mouths – during the whole song, which was item #9 –Special Music.

Item #10 was the pastoral sermon. Surely, I thought, out of the morning Scripture reading passage that is so rich in truth, there would be a resounding gospel message or a deep teaching. Scriptures like ***"living water," "Will you give me a drink?" "whoever drinks the water that I give him will never thirst,"*** and ***"God is spirit and his worshipers must worship in spirit and in truth."*** What a wealth of material!

But there was not. The theme of the message was, "Resolve to forgive others." Excuse me? Resolve to forgive others from *that* passage? What difference, I asked myself, is that message from " Do good and reach God?" As the message unfolded, I realized there was no difference. My heart ached.

I sat there thinking of the irony of it. They call this their Worship Service, the Pastor even read that God must be worshipped in Spirit and Truth – and then they proceed to worship in **ritual**. Because – that is what the 'cows' want: to do the same thing, in the same way, at the same time, in the same place. Ritual!

Occasionally, ritual for true worship can be an absolutely beautiful spiritual experience. But ritual self-destructs. It rapidly degenerates into ritual for ritual's sake! No worship offered, just going through the motions. Trying to please God by what they do…ritual, instead of circumcising the heart and worshipping Him in Spirit and Truth.

My own spirit welled within me and I fought back a terrific impulse to jump out of my seat, run down the aisle, jump on the platform, to thrust the pastor aside and shout to the people, "Let me tell you the Good News! God loves you and He gave His Son, Jesus Christ, to die for your sins so you can have eternal life! FREE! All you have to do is believe in Jesus Christ, accept Him, put your trust in Him for your salvation…and you will be born again! God loves you!"

Fireflies

But, alas, I sat glued to my seat. It was soon over. The congregation filed out, shaking hands with the minister, congratulating him on such a "fine sermon." The crowd dispersed and went their ways, until next week – same time, same place, same thing, same way…………..

CHAPTER NINE

The Garden

Self-sufficiency

Springtime bursts with activity. As the daylight hours stretch out longer and longer, they only seem to provide more time to work.

Of course, one of the major springtime activities is the garden. We try to raise a big enough garden to provide our family with enough food for the entire year. It doesn't always work out this way, but that is the goal. We have never reached total self-sufficiency from the garden because there are some things we like that will not grow in our area, but we have come close some years.

A good garden doesn't just happen. I have devised a formula for a good garden I call the "Five P" program. They are in succession;1) Plan, 2) Prepare, 3) Plant, 4) Protect, 5) Pick

The planning stage is done during the winter. Many little tidbits of information are used.

First, we do our best to estimate **family consumption** on an annual basis. This amount is usually the number of pounds estimated that the family will eat over a period of a year—that is, from harvest to harvest.

Second, we must consider **the actual size** of the garden in square footage. Just a simple calculation of length times width. Hopefully, there are no boulders or trees in the garden. The actual space sunshine strikes the fertile soil.

Third, we must take notice **the last frost date** in the spring and **the first frost date** in the fall, and the growing times of our proposed plantings.

Fourth, we need to apply **a conversion factor** that converts production in pounds per foot from each kind of vegetable and fruit into row feet, or per plant, or whatever basis needed to determine how much seed to plant in how much space.

This information is compiled over the years on more or less a trial and error basis. And we have been really good at achieving these – we have had lots of trials and lots of errors!

With these known quantities, planning becomes a matter of adjusting, increasing or decreasing last year's planting quantities; selection of varieties that do well in our area and elimination of those that do not; determining the total square footage needed and plotting the future garden on a scale plot.

Galations 6:7 "...a man reaps what he sows."

Preparation for the garden also starts in late winter. First, the chickens are turned out in there during the daylight hours for about two months to scratch and snatch all the little bugs. Then, about ten weeks ahead of our "last frost date," the garden plot is plowed with the tractor. Rotted manure is put on the soil at that time and plowed right into it.

One indoor activity at this time is to plant tomatoes and pepper seeds indoors for later transplant as seedlings.

Just prior to the "last frost date," the garden plot is

plowed again and raked smooth. Jeremiah 4:3 "...***Break up your unplowed ground, and do not sow among thorns.***"

Planting time is hectic. There is so much to do in so little time. The whole family is usually enlisted for the duration. The proper seed in the proper amounts has already been purchased. The task of planting is simply implementing "the plan" that was made in the winter. But now, it is hard work under the hot sun.

Potatoes, sweet corn, beans, tomatoes, and melons require the bulk of the garden space. After they are in, we plant the cucumbers, squashes, salad vegetables, carrots, peppers, onions, sunflowers, and on and on, seemingly ad infinitum.

In California when we lived in the mountains, our last frost date was near the end of May, but over here in the deserts of Arizona, it is usually near the end of April. In either case, by June 1st, the garden is in. We have cause to celebrate. On top of that, both my wife and my youngest daughter have birthdays on June 1st, so we usually have a Spring party.

> II Corinthians 9:6 "***Remember this: Whoever sows sparingly, will also reap sparingly; and whoever sows generously, will also reap generously.***"

Protecting the garden is an endless task. In California, we usually get no rain during the summer. Therefore, everything has to be irrigated on a rather rigid schedule. Rotted manure and worm castings are applied only once, in late June or early July, to increase the nutrients in the soil.

But the real job of protecting the garden is more than giving it food and water. The garden comes under direct attack from all sides. Gophers from below, ground squirrels or rabbits on the surface, birds and beetles from above, grasshoppers and insects from everywhere, while weeds multiply and grow quickly. A continual weeding program must be followed or they will rob the soil of its nutrients and water, choking out the vegetables.

It is a wearisome task. Just when you get one predator under control, another launches a devastating attack. It is easy to get discouraged in this stage as you watch the enemies ravish your beautiful garden.

> Galations 6:9 *"Let us not become weary in doing good: for at the proper time we will reap a harvest, if we do not give up."*

Picking or the harvest is the time I look forward to. Not because I like to pick the vegetables, but because I don't have to. After the planting, the garden is left to me. It is my responsibility during the summer months, my job to 'bring it through' to harvest. When the fruits and vegetables commence to ripen, it is the ladies in our household who gather the baskets full of tomatoes, sweet corn, squash, cucumbers, melons, beans, and all the others (they still lean on me to dig the potatoes, though.) It is best the ladies do the harvesting, for they have to process it for storage and they can set their own schedule.

> John 4:37-38 *"Thus the saying ' One sows, and another reaps is true. I sent you to reap what you have not worked for: Other have done the hard work, and you have reaped the benefits of their labor."*

One of my favorite little enjoyments of life is walking in the garden with Corinne in the summer warmth at twilight. After our evening meals, we often take our coffee and stroll through the plots and rows – not looking for anything in particular, just enjoying its progress.

My eldest daughter, Ronda, was frequently tickled by my invitation to Corinne as dinner concluded. She said it sounded so regal – like a King inviting his Queen –" Shall we stroll in the garden tonight, my dear?"

And I must admit – sometimes I do feel like a king reviewing his domain with a sense of accomplishment and admiration. During the daytime, I am the laborer – down in the soil, dirty and hot – but after dinner, and cleaned up, I switch roles.

But the thought always returns to me – I am not self-sufficient, I am totally dependent upon God! I Corinthians 3:6 **"I planted the seed, Apollos watered, but God made it grow."**

There are many, many lessons in the garden that reveal God's truth. There are lessons in the onions, in the cucumbers and melons, in the squash, in the sweet corn, lessons almost everywhere one looks. Perhaps I will write an entire book someday on God's Lessons in the Garden. But the lesson I feel led to include here concerns the radish.

Our family does not really enjoy radishes. I don't know why we even plant them each year, except we tell ourselves they add to the salad ingredients. Perhaps the real reason is that radishes germinate quicker than any other seeds we plant, so we are treated to virtually instant visual confirmation of growth activity. The radishes tend to bolster our faith and our hope that the entire garden will germinate.

> *Hebrews 11:1* **" Now faith is being sure of what we hope for, and certain of what we do not see."**

Each year there are a few radishes that are never harvested. They are pulled up on a daily basis, only as needed, and we usually over-plant to some extent, so some get left in the ground. Now, the ones that are left in the ground continue to grow until they are very large indeed. But inside, they become pithy and sharp – in a word, inedible. Then, after the radish stops growing, the tops —the leaves—start absorbing all the nourishment and grow very large. This radish is no longer suitable for the table. The ultimate disposition of these radishes reveals how God works for His glory even in adversity.

There have been many huge outreaches for Jesus Christ over the years that have apparently come to naught. Zero. A small work for Christ commences, and His workers all have their eyes on Him. Jesus blesses it, and it grows and prospers, and even flourishes. The Gospel is spread far and wide – many men and women are reached for Christ. The small work becomes a large work and continues to grow until it becomes gigantic. Chapels, radio, television, printing presses, seminaries, etc. The larger it becomes, the more money it needs to support it. The more money it needs to support it, that much more faith is required to let God produce it.

Somewhere along the line in these large, sincere, truly Gospel works that have failed, the men at the helm have lost the faith— not faith in Christ as their Savior, but faith in Christ as their Provider. They take their eyes off Jesus and start looking around for more money to continue the work. The work of spreading the Gospel becomes secondary to the work of feeding the giant organization a steady diet of money. They become pithy – inedible – and even though the work might continue for a while, all the nutrients are going into the plant, not into the fruit.

As Peter, when he was walking on the water, started to sink when he took his eyes off of Jesus – so do these great men of God and their organizations start to sink when they do the same.

Some of them did not learn the lesson of Peter walking

on the water. They sink. Their entire organization collapses, and a great work for Christ is finished. A tragic ending. Or so it seems. And it becomes easy to criticize, to find fault, and to point to failure and condemn. Don't do it!! It is not our prerogative to judge. Who knows God's overall plan, but God Himself.

Consider the radish. After the fruit has become pithy and the growth has gone to the leaves, what happens? Tiny seed pods form and as the radish dies, the pods shatter and scatter the seeds to the wind.

CHAPTER TEN

Myrtle

No one is perfect

Myrtle was our sow. We had her since she was a little weaner. To me, she epitomizes the word, 'beast.' Her noises alone are enough to frighten anyone who is unfamiliar with swine. She growls, and grunts, and barks in quite menacing ways.

The old axiom, "beauty is in the eye of the beholder," is certainly true concerning pigs. To the unappreciative eye, a hog is nothing but ugly. With its small, beady eyes, its protruding snout, its floppy, useless ear, its shapeless body, and its crinkled tail, a pig seems to have no redeeming features. But to those who have farmed, pigs are affectionately regarded as 'the mortgage lifters.'

Misconceptions

People have some misconceptions about hogs. Primarily they think pigs are dirty and dumb. Not so. Pigs are selfish and self-centered as are all other species of animals. But a pig is not stupid. In fact, a pig is quite an intelligent animal, many times more so than a sheep – which is the most stupid of all barnyard animals.

As for being dirty, a pig is really much cleaner than any other farm animal. Horses, cows, sheep, goats – all of these simply defecate wherever and whenever the urge moves them, but pigs are different. They choose a spot in their pen to use exclusively as their "bathroom." It really is quite interesting. The idea that a pig is dirty originated because pigs lie in the mud. They must! Pigs have no sweat glands, and thus have no way of keeping cool unless they wallow in the mud. In fact, a pig can die on a hot day if no water hole is provided.

A pig's diet is another area of misconception. Hogs will and do eat all kinds of garbage. They are the most efficient animals in re-cycling this kind of waste. To have healthy hogs, however, they must have substantial amounts of grain included in their diet. A pig also utilizes the 'whey' from the excess milk of the dairy cow.

Disgusting habit

The most repulsive example of a pig's efficiency is observed when it is allowed to 'co-habit' a pen with a cow or a steer who is being fed grain. The pig appears to eat the cows manure. I say " appears," because the pig does not actually eat the manure, but roots through it, looking for small particles of corn or other grain that have not been digested. When found, those are eaten by the pig. Now, *that* is real efficiency!

More Efficiency

Pigs have multiple births – like dogs and cats. It is not uncommon for a sow to have a litter of fourteen to sixteen little pigs. That too is an incredible example of efficiency. While most of the little pigs are born alive, there are usually a few which are still-born. Sometimes these little ones can be brought to life with artificial respiration, and sometimes not.

Not Needed

All little pigs are born with "needle-teeth." These are tiny razor sharp teeth in both the upper and lower jaws. They can hurt and injure the teats of some sows, but they don't seem to bother other sows. Some herdsmen practice cutting off all the babies' needle teeth right after they are born. If the sow becomes sore, she might not let the babies suck.

On the other hand, care must be taken that the needle teeth are not clipped too close to the gums of the little pig. If this is done, infection is likely to set in and the baby will not suck and obtain nourishment.

Other herdsmen decide to let nature take its course and do not clip the needle teeth. Most of the time this will work out satisfactorily with the sow. Then again, sometimes the little pigs injure each other with these teeth.

What Lessons?

What lessons has God given us with the pig? Could it be, "don't judge by looks? The pig is ugly but also the smartest, might this be true of people, too?

Or, are pigs a picture of the absolutely depraved who get their nourishment in the garbage and manure of life?

Or, are sows like evangelists who preach the gospel bringing many to Jesus – multiple births?

Or, do pigs represent those in the church who have a lowly station in life, yet are the most efficient?

Or, is the pig a portrait of a sinner who has no choice but to lie in the mud (in sin)?

Those are five lessons that could be applied to the pig. Yet there is one other.

The Needle Teeth

Just as little pigs are born with needle teeth, so are new Christians. When a person accepts Jesus Christ as his personal Savior, he is forgiven of all sin. He becomes a new person – spiritually. But he does not become perfect. He is born with imperfections.

Sometimes those imperfections are inward, people cannot see them, but nevertheless, they are still there – like the needle teeth. In others, the imperfections are outward. People can see them and everyone knows they are there. At any rate, no one is perfect just because he has been born again.

The outward imperfections are those that Christians and non-Christians alike delight in pointing to – smoking, drinking, and that sort of thing. Now these sins don't keep a person from being born again, just like needle teeth don't keep a little pig from being born.

Sometimes, our Lord, like the herdsman, reaches down and nips off these objectionable sins immediately. But other times, He seems to let nature run its course and takes care of them in His time.

Christians must learn to let the herdsman, our Lord Jesus Christ, do the clipping! Too often Christians take it upon themselves to attempt to chastise a new believer, to make the new babe feel guilty for not clipping his own needle teeth. This may result in a wounded conscience that might never heal. Too often Christians, in pompous self-righteousness, say, " Look at him – he is not born again – he still smokes!" Nonsense!

Biblical passages such as John 3:16 and Romans 10:9-10 do not put restrictions like this on salvation. Jesus said, **"What goes into a man's mouth does not make him unclean, but what comes out of his mouth, that is what makes him unclean."** *Matt 15:11*

But beware of those who have the needle teeth that cannot be seen. They are apt to injure and damage others in the litter. Gossip, criticism, judgments, envies, jealousy, strife, sowers of discord among the Church and Body of Christ. Pray for them!

CHAPTER ELEVEN

Pruning

Group Prayer

On our farm, pruning usually starts right after Christmas when all the leaves have dropped. We prune somewhat continuously all the way to spring. One chilly winter day, Corinne and I went out to prune our family orchard of deciduous fruit trees. Although pruning can actually be done at any time during the year, most of it is done in the winter while the trees are dormant. At this time, the sap is mostly in the roots. The tree in general is then best equipped to handle the shock at that time. Pruning done at other times of the year has a somewhat different effect on the growth of the plant.

In our apple orchard, we pruned all 10,000 trees to the "central leader" system. This leaves the tree looking somewhat like a Christmas tree, with a strong, straight, upward main trunk, and whorls of branches coming off at various levels. On the other hand, our family orchard gets pruned to a "vase" system, where the central leader has been removed to allow sunlight to reach the fruit on the inside of the tree.

Branches that grow the wrong way, i.e. 'into' the tree instead of 'out from' the tree, branches that have no fruit spurs, branches that hang down or cross other limbs, branches that sprout too close to the main trunk – are all targeted for removal. Snip, snip, snip, dab, dab, dab, we went through the orchard. I was cutting and she was putting on a black asphalt emulsion to seal the wound. After this targeted wood is removed, we often cut back the existing branches to a selected bud to purge the tree.

When pruning, young trees are often 'shaped' by a combination of pruning and 'spreading.' Spreading involves artificially lowering the main limb structure toward the horizontal. More on this later.

By the end of the day, we are often amazed at the amount of wood that has been cut off. The trees look bare. But the orchard was pruned – not only because it needed it, but also because the time was right.

A few years ago we had a traumatic upheaval in our little church. It resulted in the loss of our pastor and about half of the congregation. (Does that sound familiar?) However, this was not the type of split where the pastor took his faithful followers and left, but rather one where the pastor resigned over some differences in doctrine. The congregation then scattered to various other churches, not without a certain degree of bitterness and hard feelings. As our church was young and not very big at the time, we were reduced to nothing more than a couple of handfuls of people with no pastor. Why, Lord, why?

I thought of the church as it was before this upheaval. Only a handful were attending Sunday School. The Sunday morning worship service had everything in it but worship. People gathered, they sung, they listened, they were reverent. The pastor did his part: he preached, he led singing, he made announcements, and he offered communion. **But nobody worshipped!**

What a portrait of a dormant church! Dormant, not dead. There is a difference. That church was a body that was not functioning. Not dead, just not functioning. Dormant. And that is why our little church was pruned! It was in a dormant season and it needed to be pruned.

The church belongs to Jesus, and Jesus does the pruning while the Holy Spirit follows along behind and dabs the wounds with love.

But what was this little church going to do? With just a handful of members, no pastor, no building except a parsonage, what was going to happen?

I have seen some trees pruned so severely they died. They were cut back so far, there was nothing left for them to build on and survive. When springtime comes, those trees make a feeble attempt to leaf and blossom, but then they simply wither and die. Was that to be the fate of the little church?

The remaining members of that little church were advised by at least one visiting minister to merge with another local church – a denominational church. But the little group kept the faith. They knew that most trees respond to the change of season, the approach of springtime. Giving the most beautiful evidence of life – they blossom!

They also knew that before a tree is able to blossom, something else must happen. Something unseen, yet something vitally important. **The sap must flow from the roots**. *Until the sap flows, there can be no blossoms.*

Jesus Christ is our root structure. Before the little church could blossom forth to the glory of Jesus Christ, something unseen but vitally important had to happen. The sap, the power if you will, had to flow from the roots. And there is only one way for that to happen. **Prayer.** *Group Prayer. Jesus said, "* **For where two or three are gathered together in My name, there am I in the midst of them."** *Matthew 18.20 The power comes from the prayer.* **The**

presence *comes from group prayers. Prayer unlocks the power source and brings Him right into their presence.*

The little church decided to make their prayer service most important meeting of the week. And they prayed. They bonded together in a spirit of unity, and a spirit of peace. One body, praising our Lord, worshipping our Lord, and petitioning our Lord.

Spreading

Spreading is the method of laying down tree limbs from the vertical to horizontal. There are two purposes: first, to create a strong angle between the fruit bearing limb and the main trunk, so the weight of future fruit will not snap the limb. Second, for the purpose of increasing fruit production.

'Spreading' is used in apple trees. If an apple tree is simply allowed to grow wild – that is, if it is not pruned and spread, all its branches will grow upward toward the sky. Those branches will indeed produce some fruit, but their primary function will be growth. When those same branches are spread toward the horizontal, an abundance of fruit will be produced on those same limbs.

Isn't that a picture of the church? Some of the saints are prayer warriors, constantly **reaching upward** *to Jesus in prayer. Some are teachers and ministers who are reaching out* **sideways** *to their fellow man, presenting the gospel and winning souls.*

What happened to the little church?

Springtime *came to the little church. It blossomed and bore much fruit. A full-time pastor was called from clear across the continent. Souls were saved from all walks of life and joined the body. The congregation grew and grew.*

Summertime *followed. More souls were saved, and more people joined the body. Social activities abounded. Church dinners and church get-togethers were frequent. Special* *music emerged and Sunday school classes proliferated.*

Autumn *emerged as the harvest began. The Sunday services, held in the parsonage, became so crowded the little church literally exploded right out of it. They had to seek larger facilities. Sadly, somewhere along the line, the group prayer stopped. The sap stopped flowing. People were 'too busy.' The pastor and the board started quibbling over doctrine. Several got 'motes' in their eyes.*

Wintertime *inevitably followed. The little church split again and ultimately disbanded. A sad ending to a wonderful beginning. One wonders if that little church would still be viable if they had held onto their group prayer. One wonders.*

CHAPTER TWELVE

The Giant Oak

The Cathedral

We had many giant oak trees on the California ranch. They were the black oak variety, called the Encino Oak. Some of them reached over 100 feet into the sky with tremendous spread to their branches. They were really quite old as determined from the girth of their trunks. Oak trees can live to well over 100 years old. Many are documented to over 200, and a few much older than that. I like to think that perhaps these trees were just getting started at the same time our nation did. In order for oaks to survive, grow, and reproduce, they must have a reliable source of water. Large mature oak trees drink approximately 50 gallons of water daily. As we had several hundred trees on the ranch, just think of the water consumption!

Another interesting fact, scientists tell us that only one acorn in every 10,000 will grow into a mature oak tree. No wonder the tree must live so long. Acorns are not even produced by the oak tree until around 20 years of age, and increase in annual production for well over 100 years.

Most of the oaks on our ranch have a certain degree of parasitism from mistletoe. Mistletoe is a insidious plant that will keep on growing until it eventually kills the host. The tiny mistletoe seeds are highly attractive to birds who ingest them and then deposit them on the branches of other trees in their excrement. These seeds find a home in the bark of the new tree and take root. They quickly grow through the bark and place their roots in the water-conducting areas of the tree. Once they gain a foothold on the branch, there is no way to eradicate them, for their roots grow right into the limb of the tree. They become an integral part of the branch. The limb must be cut off.

One of these giant oaks near our barn had such a heavy infestation of mistletoe that it was certain to kill the tree soon. Huge clusters of great weight hung so heavily on the tree that the limbs appeared to sag. As that oak tree was probably over a hundred years old, it seemed a shame not to try to save it. The job involved three professionals – two high in the tree and one on the ground with ropes sending the chainsaw up and down as needed. It took them four hours to complete the job. They dropped limbs that we later cut into more than a full cord of firewood and a huge pile of kindling that lasted all winter long. The tree was severely pruned, but it lives today because of it.

What is the lesson? The mistletoe undoubtedly represents sin. Mistletoe brings death – sin brings death. But what is the giant tree? Is it not the old, established church? The cathedral? The giant edifice of great age in the center of town filled with people who are like cows as suggested in a previous chapter?

Of course, the church that is very old, perhaps over a hundred years old is definitely like the tree. At one time it flourished in its growth stage, but now it is large and mature. As the tree cannot defend itself from the birds who bring in the mistletoe, the large mature church cannot *defend itself against those who use the church, **but are not attached to the root source.***

Inevitably there will be those who bring in foreign seeds – innocent looking seeds, but seeds whose ultimate purpose is to destroy. The large church becomes involved in many activities in which it has no commission.

*Jesus said, "**Go into all the world and preach the good news to all creation."** Mark 16:15. This is the great commission! Every church in existence is commissioned to spread the good news, i.e. the gospel, as far and as wide as possible – both here at home and abroad. The Bible says the leaders of the church are "**… to prepare God's people for works of service, so that the body of Christ might be built up…"** Ephesians 4:12*

Yet so often the large, mature church is diverted from this commission when the innocent looking seeds appear and take root.

Social potlucks, roller skating parties, boat rides, fund raising cake sales, movies, fashion shows, bingo nights, etc. They all look innocent enough. There is nothing wrong with them – until they become functions that are ends in themselves. In other words, they are innocent until they take root in the body of Christ, the church, and start to suck the life-giving sap away from its intended purpose – that of spreading the good news of Jesus Christ.

The magnificent old church is faced then with a choice, if indeed it is even aware of its condition and that a choice is necessary. It must either decide to call upon the "gardener" (God, John 15:1) to severely prune them – or face certain death as a functioning body of Christ.

Now, if the former action is not taken, the church itself might not die, it can go on indefinitely functioning as any other social organization. But one day, it might awaken to the realization that the Spirit of God has long since departed its presence. What a pity!

CHAPTER THIRTEEN

Let's Make a Deal

Just Praise Him

Every spring we have a nice crop of new baby calves. Due to the volatility of the weather, they might be born under adverse conditions – in the snow, or in freezing rain. Occasionally one of these newborns, when exposed to these cruel elements, becomes sick and may die. Thus, it is important for the herdsman to keep an eye on his cattle, and to treat them if necessary. Sometimes we are even able to get the little ones into shelter.

We had a 40 acre pasture situated off our main working alley that we used to put the cows into just before they were to calve. Early one evening I observed a veteran cow had 'dropped' – the calf inside of her was positioning itself for birth and she was nearing her time. I opened the gate and moved her across into this 40 acre calving pasture, figuring we would probably have a calf in the morning.

And sure enough! The next morning, I checked the pasture from a distance and I saw the cow standing quietly as her new baby was attempting to nurse. One thing bothered me, though. The calf didn't look right, perhaps a little droopy. He didn't look really sick, but perhaps starting to come down with something. His ears were saggy, something about his tail didn't hang right, and he did not look like he had an abundance of energy. I made a mental note to check him later that day.

Now, I was living a perfunctory Christian life. I was teaching the adult Sunday School class, we prayed before our meals, we attended church regularly, and I was faithful to the men's prayer meetings. But there was one church activity I was not participating in, the mid-week service on Wednesday evening. This was the only evening service our church held, and I skipped it because I was milking our family cow, Elsie, every evening.

Of course, I got busy that day. The phone started ringing, there were things to do, and before I realized it the late afternoon was upon us and I had not checked the calf. It was mid-March, and we had had a snow fall a couple of days before. Most of the snow was melted, but there were patches of it here and there, usually in shade areas.

As the horses were clear up at the other end of our property, and with the day rapidly coming to a close, I simply chose to hike out to look at the calf, rather than spend the precious daylight catching my favorite horse. It was too early in the season to be concerned about rattlesnakes, one could hike without that worry.

This 40 acre field was not flat. As a matter of fact, there was a one-acre lake right in the middle, fed by a stream coming down a northern meadow. It flowed over a spillway into a gorge to another larger lake there on the property. Except for a few open areas, there were pines and oaks growing abundantly and lots of rocks and boulders on the hillsides.

Contrary to popular belief, cows do not always stay right near their calves. They tend to 'hide' their calves, and

Fireflies

then go off in search of food for themselves. Often they go so far away that they are out of visual range, but you can be sure they are within audio range of a distress call from their calf. When there are many calves, the cows might leave one of their own as a 'baby sitter.' When you try to approach one of these calves, he will bellow a warning, and mama will come running over the hill in a hurry. We try not to get that close, because the mother cow can injure her huge, engorged udder running to rescue her baby.

Cows placed in this pasture often hung out below the dam, in the grassy shaded area. I checked there first, and, sure enough, I found the mama cow. She was in good shape, contented, and grazing quietly. Good news. Her calf, more than likely, was alive and well, 'hidden' for sure, but probably fine. Nevertheless, I still needed to check him. Sometimes those mothers don't get it right, and we lose a sick calf. Scours, infection through the open navel cord, and a vast number or other maladies can strike the newborn.

I hiked and hiked. Up the hill from the dam, across the top of the east hill, criss-crossing and then down into the meadow above the lake, across the stream, down in the gullies and crevices around the lake, up the other side on the west hill, along the fence line and then back down into the area below the dam — looking, searching, scouring the countryside. Yet I found nothing!

I had no idea it was going to take such a long time to find this calf. The sun was getting low in the sky and I had the cow to milk then a school meeting to go to that night, so I felt quite a sense of urgency. I needed to find him. The only thing to do was to start again and go over the entire 40 acres once more. By this time I was asking the Lord to help me find that little guy. "Show me where to look, Lord, help me find him." No success. "Help, Lord, I need to find this little one and take care of him if he needs it." Nothing.

By the time I got down below the dam the second time,

Fireflies

the sun had gone down. We had entered into a twilight period called the 'gloaming' – a twelfth-century word meaning almost dark. And indeed, it had really gotten quite dark, but my eyes had adjusted to the lack of light and I could still see. However, I was getting exhausted. This had been a lot of fast hiking. And still, I had not found the little guy.

Finally, in frustration and resignation, I started up the hill a third time from the dam. About half way up fatigue overtook me and I stopped on the side of the hill, weary and breathing deeply.

I bowed my head and appealed to the Lord. " Lord, this is your little creature I am looking for. You love him and so do I. Please let me find him so I can check him out. We both know he didn't look well this morning. I don't know where to look anymore. I have scoured this pasture twice. Please help me."

I stood quiet for a minute with my eyes closed. Quiet prayer. Finally, I felt moved to pray, " Lord, if you will let me find this calf, I will start attending the midweek service" In other words, " Lord, let's make a deal – If you will do this – I will do that."

Battlefields over the centuries have been strewn with men who have offered these deals to the Lord. Some will testify that it worked. God did save them and bring them through the battle. But from the battlefield to the insignificant happening, isn't this a human trait? Beg God for help and offer to make a deal with Him? How many people have done this? Be honest, at some time in your life, haven't you tried to make a deal with God? Whether it be a life and death matter like on a battle field, or a seemingly inconsequential matter like finding a calf?

I was totally surprised and shocked when almost immediately upon uttering "the deal" I was offering to the Lord, I felt surrounded — **by a mysterious pressure.** That is the only way I can describe it. I felt like I was being squeezed on all sides. The pressure compressed me so tightly I was having trouble catching my breath. I repeatedly gasped. It frightened me. What was happening?

I did not hear an audible voice. About the only way I can describe what happened then is that I experienced a consciousness – a thought that was not coming from me, that was actually foreign to my mind-set. This thought emblazoned across my mind while I was struggling to breathe, **"How dare you try to make a deal with the Living God?"**

I was stunned and confused. I realized what I had done, and realized how wrong it was. That's all wrong! God doesn't want us to offer deals to Him. Especially deals we are likely not to keep. Of course not. What does He want? What does God want? Strange yet interesting, while still under that pressure surrounding me, I remembered a testimony given by a commercial fisherman who detailed how God had worked with him out in the ocean when this fisherman gave God what He really wants from us.

It flashed on my mind, ***"Just praise the Lord."*** And that is what I did. I actually said aloud, " Pardon me, Sir, I am sorry for what I did, please forgive me, I really have no right nor business to do anything but to praise you and thank you for all your goodness to us. Praise you, Lord Jesus."

Instantly, the pressure lifted. I know this sounds incredible, but this is exactly what happened! I kept praising Him. By this time, tears were running down my face. And then the most astounding thing happened. I can seldom recall this scene without becoming emotional. As I opened my tear-filled eyes there in the gloaming – almost totally dark now – *without moving my feet*, it was as if an invisible hand immediately rotated my head about 30 degrees to the right and directed it downward. My eyes widened and bulged, and I jumped with a start as I saw movement there in a tiny lump of snow up under a bush — blink! Two eyes blinked at me! It wasn't snow! It was the white face of our new calf, lying quietly watching me. Goose bumps came up on my arms and the hair on the back of my neck raised! I was looking at my calf!

Of course, God knew where that calf was all the time. And God brought me up the hill, stopped me with fatigue right in front of that calf, and then blinded me so that I could not see him in the gloaming...until after He had dealt with me. Think of it.

I went back out there the next day and carefully measured approximately 8 feet, from my eyeballs to where the calf's head was. I had walked by that spot several times in my search. Please realize that I believe the calf was there all the time. Don't think I am suggesting that God performed a miracle of transposition movement. In other words, I do not believe for a minute that God picked that calf up somewhere else and deposited him there right in front of me. I simply believe God prevented me from seeing the calf until He was ready for me to see it; and at the same time prevented me from coming too close to that calf where he would have bawled for his mother. God directed my path up that particular way on the hill, and then stopped me in just the right position, the right distance, the right time, and facing the right direction.

What more is there to say, but **PRAISE THE LORD!** Oh, I almost forgot – I checked the calf out through my tears and the calf was in good health, he was fine. God knows your problems, God knows your inadequacies, and God knows your heart. Just praise Him! You will be blessed.

I hurriedly stumbled home in the dark to tell my wife what had happened.

CHAPTER FOURTEEN

The Mower

Keep on Praising Him

One spring, Corinne and I decided to make a motor trip to Iowa and Michigan. Of course, our over-riding concerns were our home and our farm. I managed to solve the temporary disposition of all our animals, but still had the nagging problem of leaving our home unattended for over a month .

We tried various people whom we thought might be interested but with no luck. The more we tried, it seemed like the less interest we could develop in such a plan. That was a little ironic because we had a lovely home with a lovely view, and a beautiful piece of property with lakes to swim and fish in. It didn't make sense to us.

Corinne had some necessary reasons for making this trip, in addition to not having seen her people for seven years. It was important that we go, but we were blocked. We decided to seek God's will in this matter and prayed about it not a little bit. The summer was approaching fast and the matter was not settled. We finally just gave up, deciding that

Fireflies

if God wanted us to go, He would provide – otherwise, we would stay home. In the meantime, our pastor called a couple of missionary organizations and informed them of the availability of our home.

One evening the phone rang and a retired missionary was on the line, wanting to take our home for the time we were to be gone. He had been a pilot for Wycliffe Bible Translators in Columbia and his wife had worked with him as a nurse. He had to return home due to his health, but was working in the main office of Wycliffe. As this call seemed a direct answer to prayer, we made the deal right on the phone. It was no mistake. God had provided.

Preparations for shutting down activity and leaving a farm for a month are more than one realizes. And to complicate things, most of it is all last-minute details.

All the old hens were killed and put in the freezer, we would start with new ones when we returned. The pig, our gilt, was taken down to a boar to be bred and boarded until we returned. Our sheep were taken down to a ram to be boarded. Our milk cow, Elsie, had to be dried up and turned out in the pasture with the beef cattle. All the cattle had to be treated with insecticide almost at the last minute. The horses had to be shifted to a pasture with natural water in it. The lamb and the beef steer had to be slaughtered and put in the freezer. The berries had to be harvested and frozen. The barn with all of our equipment and tools had to be boarded up and secured.

The garden required the most work. As the missionary was going to take care of our garden and orchard while we were gone, I felt I had to have it in absolutely top shape condition when he arrived. I spent hours in the garden doing so. (Actually, I was doing what I have often laughed at my wife for doing – cleaning house before the housecleaner arrives).

Then a kink developed in our plans. About ten days

Fireflies

before departure, our dog Ringo started limping. We examined his paws and pulled out a couple of foxtails. But his limping got worse, and within 48 hours he had a high fever and could not even walk. Both of his hind-legs were helpless. After examination, the veterinarian explained to me that the dog would have to be operated on. Horrors! What timing! But the operation was done, and Ringo was brought home to convalesce.

During this time, I kept pecking away at the long list of chores and accomplishments that needed to be finished before departure. One of them was to mow the acre out front to knock down the fire hazard of the tall weeds. The California mountains receive most of their rainfall in the winter and early spring. The fields and meadows are green during the spring months, and turn golden in early June. By mid-July they are dry and brown.

Our mower is a heavy, large-wheeled, geared, walk-behind tractor driven by a small gasoline engine with a pull-rope starter. I finally got to the mower one afternoon about 1:30. I tried to start the machine time and again, until I was simply beside myself in sweat, in frustration, and my own ineptitude. I was not blessed with an abundance of patience when my personality was molded. And, I might add that, I am so gifted mechanically that I almost need an instruction manual to put gasoline in the car.

The scorching sun was dragging the energy out of me and this machine just would not run. Finally, I gave up. I felt like cursing the machine out, and pounding it with a hammer, but I restrained myself. In utter resignation and surrender, I dropped to my knees by the mower and said a simple prayer, something to the effect of,

"Lord, I know this mower is out of adjustment, and You know I don't know the least little thing about adjusting it. Now, whatever happens, I am just going to praise you. If you want me to mow this field, then show me how to adjust the mower. If you don't want me to mow it, then it wont run. Either way I'll just praise you."

I got up and set all the adjustments to zero – carburetor fuel and air valves. Then I took the screw driver in my hand and just stood there looking at it a moment, trying to empty myself and concentrate on letting the Lord guide me. Then I proceeded to make a certain amount of turns on each of them. I stood back and took a deep breath, and pulled on the starter lanyard.

WHAROOOM!!!!! The engine roared to life.

The engine ran a few seconds and died. Well, praise the Lord! I pulled again. And again the engine fired to life, only to die again. I pulled the cord a third time, and a third time the engine started, but this time as it started to die, I audibly said, " Praise the Lord." The engine did not die! It zoomed alive and kept running.

I engaged the clutch and started down the 600 foot drive. Now this part is simply amazing. Every fifty or sixty feet down the drive, the engine started to die. Each time it got down to its last chug, chug, I said, "Praise the Lord" and each time the engine roared back to life again! This happened nine or ten times. It seemed incredible!

When I reached the end of the 600 foot drive and swung the mower toward the open space, I felt that still, small voice inside me say to me,

"Now that you know who is making your mower run, go ahead and mow your field."

From that moment on, that engine actually hummed and purred without skipping a beat for the next two and a half hours. I shut it down twice, once to go get a cold drink, another time to refuel, and each time it started on the first pull and commenced humming again. It did not die even once, or even act like it was going to die.

Some of this mowing was on the side of a hill, and some of it was around some large trees, all of it had tall weeds. By the time I had finished I was nearly exhausted, but I decided to do a little trimming around the edges and some cosmetic cutting here and there to make it look nice. Not necessary, but nice.

I stumbled and fell a couple of times from fatigue, but stayed with the machine. Only a very few minutes went by until the mower abruptly stopped. I tried to start it. Nothing. Tried again. Nothing. Without kneeling or even bowing, I just talked to the Lord, "Lord, you know I would like to finish this, but if you say I'm done, well, praise the Lord, I'm done. Anyway, I'm bushed! But if you want me to finish this, please start it." I checked the fuel and the oil. Both full. Pulled the starter. No. Once more, no start.

Then I looked up and saw my daughter Robin walking toward me. Actually she was quite close by this time, and she said, "Dad, it's time to quit, we have to bring in the cows." I turned my head so she wouldn't see the tears in my eyes.

Two Months Later

There is a sequel to this story. From the day that mower finally stopped in early July, no attempt was made to run it again until early September. On that day, I asked my son if he would do some mowing while I was in town. When I returned, the mowing had not been done. As I came into the house, he walked over and asked me what was wrong with the mower. I answered his question with a question, "Why?"

Rick said that he could not get it to run, that it was horribly out of adjustment, and that he spent two hours trying without success. I should add here that Rick is mechanically inclined and even though still a high school student, he knew his way around machines. That statement confirmed my experience. I know who made the mower run for me. Machines don't fix themselves. That mower wasn't going to run again until it was properly adjusted.

Nevertheless, the mower had run for me. It had run not because it was properly adjusted, not because it was 'dieseling' (it wasn't), but because God wanted to teach me a lesson. Attempts might be made to explain this experience away as a natural phenomenon. I too have been skeptical in the past when I have heard people say, "God did this" or "God told me that," but this happened to me. And I know exactly how it happened. There were too many coincidences in sequence, the mathematical odds are against anything natural. It was indeed supernatural. It was a spiritual experience.

CHAPTER FIFTEEN

Noah's Ark

God provides a way

I wish they would find Noah's Ark. Intact. It would answer many questions in my mind about that episode. I am aware of some of the progress in this area in the past century, the various sightings on Mt. Ararat, the various expeditions, and the testimony of the man who claims he touched it.

I have a keen interest in its construction. I would be fascinated to see exactly how it was put together and especially how it was internally arranged.

Ponder, if you will, on some of the implications of the story of the Ark. Many folks mentally picture Noah and his family sitting in circle, holding hands and praising God for saving them, floating along in blissful safety while the storm raged outside. No doubt they did do this, but you can be sure that wasn't all they did.

The Bible says, *"You are to take every kind of food that is to be eaten and store it away as food for you and for them."* Genesis 6:21. Think about that! Noah gathered enough food for his family and the animals to last them for over a year. Check on it. They were in the Ark for over a year. However, the food supply was not the major problem. Noah and his sons had plenty of time to gather and store food before the flood.

It is not known how many animals went aboard. The Bible says Noah took seven pairs of each species of clean animals, and one pair of each of the unclean. The possibilities in actual numbers fall in a range from 7,000 animals to over 50,000 animals, depending upon exactly how they were grouped, i.e. what constituted a specie. This is a vast study in itself, with many hard questions inherent therein, but regardless of the number of animals within that range, the Ark was sufficiently large in size to accommodate them. Anyone can do the mathematics.

But how did the animals get fed? Were they in cages or were they loose? Did Noah and his family have to distribute food on a daily or twice-daily basis? Did the carnivores have to eat fresh meat? Did God intervene in the diet of the carnivores to let them crave and subsist on grain or grass? Anyone who has ever fed animals knows what a big chore it is to feed several hundred animals each day, let alone several thousand— and to do it without any mechanical equipment. Perhaps the Ark was constructed and subsequently loaded in such manner as to facilitate ease of feeding.

And how were the animals watered? I have read Old Testament commentators who have dismissed the water problems with hardly a thought. They seemed to think that because it rained there was plenty of fresh water. Maybe it did rain enough; at sufficient intervals (daily?)for over a year, but how was the water collected and how was it distributed? The mechanics of watering that many animals, even if they were allowed free choice to a common reservoir or basin, are staggering.

Fireflies

The major problem on the Ark

Both the feed and water problem are miniscule compared to that of refuse disposal. One thing is apparent, God did not suspend normal bodily functions. If the animals ate and drank, then they produced refuse – manure and urine if you will. The number of animals that naturally hibernate, like the bear, are few.

Now here is a staggering fact, and one that I wouldn't have been aware of had I not worked with animals.

Animals typically produce between 10 to 20 times their own body weight in manure each year!

- A dairy cow produces 15 tons of manure in a year.
- A horse, the light riding type, produces 10 tons of manure a year.
- Seven sheep produce seven and a half tons of manure a year.
- Two mature hogs will produce 12 tons of manure a year.

The refuse problem was gigantic problem indeed! And this problem must be considered from both the standpoints of added weight and bulk.

The added weight is not as big a problem as it might seem. A cow, or horse, will eat approximately 12 times its body weight in food during a year. The added weight of the manure is, of course, water. The Ark only floated 150 days (5 months). Then it settled on the surface of the earth for the next seven and a half months while they were still inside waiting for the waters to subside. Any added weight from the manure during the five months afloat probably was not significant in regards to flotation. Mathematical calculations show no critical problems in added weight as far as center of gravity shifts.

But there would have been a bulk problem. What

happened to the manure? Either it stayed aboard or it was shoveled out. If it was shoveled out, i.e. dumped over the side from the windows, Noah and his sons had tremendous daily tasks. They would have worked from dawn until dusk, every day in feeding, watering, and then cleaning up the manure, gathering it, and lifting it by means of crude shovel out the windows. Tons of it every day. They might have done this, but I don't believe they had to. If they did have to do this, we get a picture of Noah and his sons working regularly and feverishly during their adventure. Initially, I thought that concept would be inconsistent with New Testament teaching, but on second thought, I realize that it is not.

Undoubtedly, the Ark is a type of Christ. All theologians generally accept this. Once inside Christ (the Ark) people are safe, they are secure. But they are not to sit down and continue sitting there, doing nothing. They have tremendous tasks to perform and keep on performing.

The question is NOT whether the Ark would fill up with manure and capsize or sink if the refuse were not removed. If this were the case, then Noah and his family would have been *working* for their own salvation. This cannot be done and absolutely contrary to New Testament teaching.

> *"For it is by grace are you have been saved, through faith— and this not from your- selves: it is the gift of God— not by works, so that no one can boast." Ephesians 2: 8-9*

The question and problem revolves around whether Noah and his family had to constantly work in the Ark: Not for their salvation, not for fear of the ship sinking, but for the well-being of the animals in which they were entrusted. I believe they did.

But whether the manure was shoveled out, or whether it was gathered and moved to another location within the Ark,

I do feel that it was indeed taken care of in one of these ways. I cannot believe that either God or Noah would allow their animals to live and sleep in their own and each other's excrement. I have seen both calves and pigs raised this way and the results are repulsive. The animals lie in their own manure, it becomes caked on their bodies and all over their heads and faces, they become susceptible to disease, and it a disgusting situation all the way around. I also cannot believe that the animals were "trained to go to the bathroom." Anyone who has ever been around large animals knows how ridiculous that is.

Modern Methods

In the last fifty years, hog farmers and cattle feeders have taken to raising and feeding their animals in constant indoor confinement. Just like the Ark. Many pigs, raised in these houses, never see the light of day from the time they are born until the day they are shipped. These pig houses and cattle sheds are constructed with slatted, concrete floors that allow the manure to be trampled through slats to an area below where the manure collects and is subsequently removed.

Perhaps God showed Noah how to build the floor of the animal deck with slats for the manure to be trampled down, a technique that was not discovered for thousands of years later. Perhaps. But that raises other questions. Was the animal deck the bottom deck? If so, were bilges there under it, or was the floor of the third deck actually the bottom of the ship? That raises the question, how was the Ark loaded? We can only speculate that the top two decks were filled with feed, because of its enormous bulk, and the bottom deck carried the animals. I can't imagine animals above the feed. If so, did Noah get an absolutely perfect seal on the floors of the decks. If not, the feed below would have been contaminated with urine, and perhaps even manure. Each question seems to open up avenues for more questions.

Interesting Possibility

Several years ago I started a worm-raising program on the ranch. I built several worm beds and raised them for cash sale, mostly to retailers for fishing bait and castings. At various intervals, we would 'harvest' forty, fifty, sixty pounds of worms a day that were wholesaled out.

There are many different kinds of worms, but the easiest to raise "in captivity" and the most prolific are the *red worms*. They are not earthworms, but in reality, manure worms. They live, eat, and breed in manure.

Here comes the interesting part. Sexually, the worms are hermaphroditic. That is, each worm produces both male sperm and female eggs. Nevertheless, it takes two worms to breed – they breed each other and then both of them lay eggs or capsules. Each worm will lay two to four capsules a month. Each capsule will contain two to twenty baby worms inside it. It takes those hatching baby worms about four months to become breeders themselves. You can do the arithmetic, but even without doing it you can imagine the incredible population explosion of these worms! As a very conservative rule of thumb (allowing for every kind of problem) worms will double their population every 30 days. Theoretically speaking, a bin of 100,000 worms (about 100 lbs) will breed to over 400 million worms in a year.

Practically speaking, the population explosion on a worm farm is not quite that fast. It tends to slow up due to (1) "picking" mature worms for shipment; thus reducing breeder worms; (2) sale of castings, i.e. a shovel full of the worm bed itself containing thousands of capsules; and (3) "crawl" —a condition that results when the worm beds become overcrowded or too wet. Many worms simply tend to crawl out of the beds and leave, often straight up the sides of the walls if they are inside a building. I have witnessed this phenomenon on many occasions. They can go right through joints in a building. Here is an interesting story about this.

Once we received an order to ship several pounds of live worms to a resort in New England. We packaged them in a tightly sealed box and scheduled it straight through to its destination. The box never arrived! The purchaser contacted us and questioned. So we put a tracer on the box. What a comical story we received in return. Somehow, the box was set off the plane in Chicago where it sat for a couple of days. Someone noticed worms crawling out of the box and all over the floor, other boxes, the walls, everywhere! The employees were afraid to touch it, so just left it in a corner of the warehouse. How did the worms get out of the tightly sealed box? They can just about go through anything.

Important Facts

There are a half dozen other characteristics of Red Worms that are worth noting here. First, they love darkness and detest light. Second, they will eat virtually any 'kind' of manure. It makes little difference to them from what animal it came. Third, as worms ingest the manure, they virtually obliterate the smell. There are no vile odors from worm beds. Fourth, chickens love to eat these worms. As the worms are almost 60% protein, the addition of worms to a chicken's diet enriches its eggs. Our chickens are given access to the worm beds in the wintertime, and they almost go insane with delight – clucking, scratching and pecking their hearts out. Fifth, worms do no damage to wood - the material from which the Ark was constructed would have been unaffected. And sixth, as worms eat their way through a pile of manure, they reduce the bulk by over two-thirds. In other words, a three-foot pile of manure, when completely ingested, digested, and expelled from the worms, becomes a one-foot pile of castings.

I could build quite a case for a type of Satan in the red worm. You might go through these six characteristics and build a Satan teaching, i.e. loves darkness, eats any kind of filth, makes sin alluring (de-odorizing) etc.

What happened on the Ark?

No one is really sure. Further, I doubt that many people even think about it. Doesn't seem important. But for some reason, I have thought about it a lot and the more I do, the more I become convinced that in all likelihood Noah did not have to throw all the manure overboard – a virtually impossible task to keep up with. I think it is reasonable to assume and is more likely that Noah and his sons had to clean stalls and transport indiscriminately-dropped manure to various "drops" or chute locations where it plunged below to active worm beds. Down there, the continuously eating worms would reduce the bulk of it, keeping everything in balance. The piles would logically be located far below decks, in the dark, which the worms love. And when the piles become over-populated, the worms would crawl right up the walls, through the joints and cracks into the next upper deck where they would become delicious morsels for the birds, chickens, and other fowl.

Yes, Noah and his family had to work— hard work, physical work, never-ending work. But their work was of the nature of a pastor. Jesus said, "Feed my sheep," and Noah literally fed the sheep and all the other animals in the safety of the ark. Noah also moved and removed the manure – not because their salvation depended on it, but because their sanitation and well-being depended upon it. In the same vein, pastors are constantly dealing with the ugly problems of life among their flock.

But it was God who provided a way for the 'impossible' task – that of constantly decreasing the bulk of the refuse and de-fusing its offensiveness. And finally, out of the manure pile and trash, came more food for some of the inhabitants of the Ark. God can use even the hideous and repulsive to provide for His Own. ***Praise the Lord!***

CHAPTER SIXTEEN

The Raccoon

Thief in the night!

"**W**ake up! I hear something happening up at the chicken pen," Corinne whispered urgently as she shook my arm. My body was tired, my head was groggy – I had been up all night the night before – and my eyes were still asleep. But slowly I came to consciousness as she continued to nudge me and whisper in my ear.

I listened. Indeed, something was going on up at the hen house. The squawking was neither shrill nor urgent, but sounded more like a chicken in agony. I swung my legs out of bed and reached for my clothes with a deep sigh of fatigue – it was 3:45AM.

About every third or fourth morning for the preceding month, we would find a dead hen in the chicken yard. Sometimes the body was intact; others, the neck had been broken and chewed through; still others had leg or wing missing; and still others had half their body missing. We could not identify our marauder. Was it a weasel? Was it a hawk? Dogs? What could be getting our chickens?

The chicken thief stepped up his visits to nightly. I

decided to stake out. So, in the evening, I took a chair, flashlight, and a shotgun; stationed myself about fifty feet away from the chicken pen and sat up in the dark, all night long. Nothing happened. That was last night. No wonder I felt so groggy right now.

I pulled on my boots, quickly grabbed the flashlight and stumbled out into the dark, moonless night. I kept the flashlight shining on the ground in front of me lest I step on a rattlesnake. About thirty feet from the chicken house, I stopped and listened. I determined the exact position of the sound and quickly flashed my beam over there.

There he was! The biggest, fattest, furriest raccoon I had ever seen in my life. He was holding and chewing on a chicken. But rats! I had forgotten my shotgun. All I could do was scare him away. At least we now knew who was killing the chickens.

The next night, the raccoon was back again. Chickens sleep so soundly on their roost that anyone can walk right up to them and grab them. The raccoon got another one, and the hen started to squawk. Corinne woke me again, and this time I grabbed the gun and went on the run.

The raccoon ran too. I tried to hold the flashlight on a moving target with my left hand and to aim and fire with my right hand. Hard enough to do with a stationary target, virtually impossible with a moving one. I got off two shots, but missed them both.

I might add parenthetically here that in an earlier chapter I said, "…killing non-threatening living creatures is not my thing." That's true, but when wild animals invade our space and start killing our livestock or eating our food supply, they become targets.

I realized the only way our chickens would be and could be secure was to enclose the hen house and its immediate yard so tightly that nothing could crawl in or out. I worked on that most of the day.

The raccoon never got another chicken.

The lesson is really a simple one. Without getting into the great Calvanistic-Armenian controversy of Eternal Security that debates the possibilities of one who has been saved then being ultimately lost – let's just consider the chicken coop.

The chickens inside have roosted and sleep in faith and trust. They have placed their trust in their resting place. They are utterly defenseless when they sleep. Their total defense lies not in their awareness, nor in their fighting ability – but in the security of the coop itself.

*The world is full of people who have placed their faith and trust in insecure chicken coops. They roost and sleep believing they are safe in Islam, Buddhism, or other religions. Or they have placed their faith in cults, in money, in power, or their own ability. But they have no **living** keepers. Their gods are all dead. Nightly, without fail, the marauder takes them one by one to their eternal death.*

As Christians, we have placed our faith and trust in our resting-place, our Lord Jesus Christ. We are utterly defenseless on our own against the marauder, the Evil one. Our total defense lies not in our awareness, nor in our combat ability – but in the security of our Lord. We are safe, because Jesus is alive and He has promised us security.

> **"But whoever listens to me will live in safety and be at ease, without fear of harm."**
> *Proverbs 1:33*

The Apostle Paul confirms this. **"For I am convinced that neither death nor life, neither angels nor demons, neither the present nor the future, nor any powers, neither height nor depth, nor anything else in all creation, will be able to separate us from the love of God that is in Christ Jesus our Lord."** *Romans 8:38-39*

CHAPTER SEVENTEEN

Calving

Some need help!

Most cows give birth naturally. We've talked about that earlier. Watching a normal birth is a fascinating experience. The first evidence of the baby's imminent birth is two tiny hooves, front feet, protruding from the mother. Shortly, the nose follows, then the entire head, the shoulders, the body, the hips, and the back legs. The entire birth doesn't really take very long, just a matter of minutes, but it always seems like it is taking an unconscionable amount of time. Usually, when a baby is about half-born, i.e. half-expelled from his mother, the navel cord breaks. The delicate cord is severed when the middle of his body passes across the mother's pelvic bone. Often the baby gives an involuntary gasp at this point and starts to breathe.

It is the same way with the new birth! A person comes to Jesus Christ first with **outstretched hands** *– willingness. Next comes the* **head** *– mental assent and belief – followed by the* **heart**, *placing full faith and trust in Christ. And as soon as the heart is exposed and placed in Jesus' domain,* *the baby breathes new life. It naturally follows that the entire body is brought forth – the baby's entire life is delivered to Christ.*

Concerning cattle births, I have learned one thing the hard way: be prepared for anything to happen! That simply means, have the right equipment handy, have the proper supplies on hand, and be studied up on some of the infrequently used, but necessary procedures. Occasionally, these make the difference between life and death.

Actual birth problems are of two basic types. The first type concerns the size of the calf and the cow in relation to each other. The head, and/or the shoulders, and/or the hips of the calf may be too large for normal passage through the birth canal. Or to look at it another way, the cow is too small to accommodate the normal passage of the calf. However one looks at it, assistance is necessary.

The second type of birth problem results from improper positioning of the calf within the cow. There are many variations to this problem. A calf can be improperly positioned for birth in many different ways. One of the most common ways is the breech where the calf is positioned backwards and is born hind feet first. Other ways include one or both of the front legs folded backwards or turned under; or once in a while a calf's head might be turned to the side. All of these abnormalities prevent passage of the calf through the birth canal. But most of them are relatively infrequent, and we praise the Lord that they are!

Permit me to include a parenthetical thought here. Most people are disoriented concerning birth abnormalities. They tend to focus their attention on the tragedy of the abnormality. And indeed, it is a tragedy, especially if it is fatal and happens to you. I am talking about birth abnormalities now, and not birth defects or deformities. My only son was born with his naval cord wrapped around his neck so tightly it was threatening his very life. At precisely the same time, his mother started to die. The doctor and his assistants had a double emergency! That morning the medical team enjoyed a double success as both mother and son were brought through alive. But later, the doctor, who was personal friend, told me confidentially that during the emergency he indeed thought he was going to lose them both, and he was already thinking about what he was going to tell me!

But the wonder of wonders...the miracle...is that so many babies are born normally! An inordinate, unbelievably high-percentage of them are born without incident.

Regardless of how the baby is improperly positioned, it must be re-positioned before birth can be accomplished. This is not true of the "breech," it will be dealt with later. It is up to the herdsman to reach in through the birth canal, determine exactly what is wrong, and then manipulate the turned or doubled-under part into the correct position. Then, the baby can be born naturally.

The "breech" poses another problem. Frequently the mother needs no assistance in expelling the baby, but the baby is often dead. For the same reason that a normal baby often breathes before he is totally born, the breech does so while his head is still deep inside his mother. If the birth is quite fast, sometimes those babies can be saved. Any kind of delay or slow birthing procedure, however, and the calf either drowns or suffocates. To further complicate matters, once in awhile during a breech birth, the tail or one of the feet 'hang up' in the birth canal preventing passage. This almost assures the death of the calf.

Actual birth problems of individuals about to experience the new birth are of two basic types that, like cattle, concern size and position.

One type of individual is hung up on **size**. *He says, "I am too great a sinner, God would never forgive and accept me." His perspective is wrong. Great sinners are those whom Christ came to save.*

*The Apostle Paul said, " **Here is a trustworthy saying that deserves full acceptance: Christ Jesus came into the world to save sinners – of whom I am the worst." I Tim. 1:15***

The greater the sinner, the greater the testimony. Jesus accepted Paul – an accessory to murder and prosecutor of Christians. Jesus accepted Eldrege Cleaver, former leader of the Black Panthers; He accepted Charles Colson, key Watergate figure. He will accept you, too.

The second category has to do with improper positioning. The position must be changed before birth can be accomplished.

There are those who see no need in being born again.

They feel they "have lived a good life, obeyed the Ten Commandments as best they could, and can acquit themselves quite well before God, thank you."

But the Bible indicates differently.

> *"Know that a man is not justified by observing the law, but by the faith in Jesus Christ...because by the law no man will be justified." Gal 2:16*
>
> *"You are the ones who justify yourselves in the eyes of men; but God knows your hearts. What is highly valued among men is detestable in God's sight." Luke 16:15*

"I have tried this before and it didn't work."

It is difficult to know exactly what happened before without asking, "why?" The position must be determined before help can be given. In this case, the problem is probably either one of two things:

(1) *The individual 'believed' but did not 'receive.' He did not follow through his belief with a reception of Jesus Christ as his Lord and Master by putting his full faith and trust in Him.*

> **"Yet to all who received him, to those who believed on his name, he gave the right to become children of God." John 1:12**

(2) The person was indeed born again but turned away from Christ for one reason or another. This person is often called a backslider. Whatever he is, he should consider two verses of scripture.

> **"If we confess our sins, he is faithful and just and will forgive us our sins and purify us from all unrighteousness". I John 1:9**

> **"If my people who are called by my name will humble themselves and pray and seek my face and turn from their wicked ways, then will I hear from heaven and will forgive their sins and will heal their land."** II Chronicles 7:14

Finally, there are those who try to back into salvation.

They try to take it upon themselves to become a better person before they can become a Christian. They think they need to clean up their life before Christ will accept them.

Nothing can be farther from the truth. This will not work. It inevitably leads to nothing – a still born. Still dead. People need to open their hearts and accept Jesus Christ as they are – with no conditions, a total commitment – not as they would like to be.

"But God demonstrates his own love for us in this, while we were still sinners, Christ died for us." Romans 5:8

Breakfast

Do you remember Howie, the little calf in an earlier chapter who had to be pulled into this world? His story did not end with his birth. There were problems that seem to go along with many calves who are pulled.

For one, this experience was a new dimension for Howie's mother, and an unpleasant one at that. The little heifer reacted in fear. She jumped up and ran off into the darkness. We backed away into the darkness also, hoping she would return to the calf if we were not there. She didn't. So we put little Howie in a large corral near the barn, and finally succeded in chasing Mama in there also. We locked them in together.

Poor little mama had conflict. Her maternal instinct was fighting her fear instinct. She was drawn to the baby, would go over to him and sniff, but then would become frightened when he responded in movement.

As it was now 12:45 AM, I had Corinne and Rick return to the house, but decided I had better stay until Howie had taken his breakfast. He never did. He tried for three hours to get up, but each time he fought and struggled to his feet, his mama would get excited and mistakenly knock him down.

Howie's front legs were either temporarily injured, or sore from the strain of the chains on his legs during birth. It seemed painful for him to use those front legs, as though it hurt for him to stand up.

It began to rain. Howie's efforts became more feeble, and farther apart. His vitality seemed to be going down hill rapidly. His mother had not licked him clean, as is a cow's natural custom. Howie was still wet and starting to shiver in the cold rain. It became evident some help was needed.

Fireflies

At 3:45AM, I returned to the house and aroused Corinne. I just didn't have the heart to awaken Rick. Anyway, the two of us moved the cow and the calf down to the working corral in the rain, put the mother in the squeeze, and locked her in. Then we held Howie up to his mama so he could get his first breakfast. And was he hungry! He ate like he had never had anything to eat in his life!

When he had finished, we dried him off with towels and rubbed him vigorously to stimulate him. We put them both in a nice, dry stall in the barn to spend the night on fresh straw. It was 5:15 in the morning. It seemed too late to go to bed, so we returned to the house and Corinne fixed a gigantic, super breakfast. We celebrated and rejoiced. We, too, ate like we had never had anything to eat in our lives!

Howie's problems of soreness or injury during birth that made it difficult for him to rise, stand, and nurse, are not the only problems encountered shortly after birth. We have had problems and/or lost calves due to exposure to weather extremes; rejection of the baby by its mother; being born in unsafe places, and falling off a cliff or falling into a lake; and many others.

*And as Howie had problems shortly after his birth, so do many new Christians. Their problems often result from **fear, anxiety, and injury.***

Fear *is a big problem because it is frequently concerned with misconception, a failure to perform. Many new Christians mistakenly believe they have ' to be' Christians instead of recognizing 'they are' Christians. They have fears that they cannot live up to Christian standards. But any failure they might have, is not the result of not living up to the Christian life, but in understanding Romans 8:1* **"Therefore there is now no condemnation for those who are in Christ Jesus."**

Anxieties *usually center on worries concerning their families and friends. The fact that they do worry about their*

Christian witness is a good sign. There are far too many 'closet Christians' who have no witness at all except perhaps in church. They must realize that whatever happens, God **will keep you "in perfect peace, him whose mind is steadfast, because he trusts in you"** *Isaiah 26:3*

Injuries *are inevitable. Family, friends, business acquaintances are going to turn away from the new Christian. It will hurt. Especially when you are rebuffed trying to present the Good News to a friend.* **"In fact, everyone who wants to live a godly life in Christ Jesus will be persecuted ."** *II Timothy 3:12 Not a very encouraging prospect. But Jesus died for you!*

New babies often have a critical time shortly after their birth. Christians, be alert, they might need assistance at this time. After all the rejoicing and testifying, the new babe might encounter deep trouble. He or she needs your help, your friendship, your love, your care, your prayers, your advice, your guidance, perhaps more at that time than any other period of the spiritual life. We all know of cases where lives have been dramatically changed when the new birth is experienced. But in others, the change is only inward. The joy of the Lord is experienced, but joy is an emotion that is subject to ebb and flow. When the joy ebbs, as it inevitably will do, discouragement is apt to set in, making it harder for the babe to stand up again.

Are you prepared to help?

CHAPTER EIGHTEEN

The Pear Tree

Fruit!

We had a large, beautiful twenty-year old pear tree in our 55 tree family orchard. It has been a delight to us until about five years ago. At that time, it blossomed in the springtime and set a copious abundance of fruit as it always had in the past. But something happened that year – the fruit never matured. It hardened. The pears just gnarled and refused to ripen, both on and off the tree. It was a puzzle to us, but the pressures of running businesses and the farm diverted our minds from it until it was simply forgotten.

The following year, the same thing happened. And again, we did nothing about it. Now the third year, this tree was covered with beautiful blossoms, and the fruit set was very heavy. We thought, "Surely this year the fruit will be edible." But it was not, it repeated the same syndrome of the previous years. So, while the hardened, gnarled fruit was still hanging on the tree, I called in an expert orchard man and asked him to evaluate this tree. He examined the tree thoroughly, tested the fruit, scrutinized the leaves and the bark, and came away shaking his head. He told me that he had no idea what was wrong with this tree, and could not explain the peculiar development of the fruit that left it immature, hard, and inedible.

The following year was simply a repeat of the previous three. I resolved to prune that tree severely the next winter to shock it, thinking perhaps the jolt of a severe pruning might snap it out of it's problem. But alas, the winter turned to springtime so fast that next year the job didn't get done.

As springtime cascaded in overwhelming the winter that year, fifty-four trees in our family orchard blossomed profusely and set fruit. But this particular pear tree did not set one pear. It was barren. It leafed out in a splendor of beauty, but it was barren. I realized that something had changed and considered that whatever was wrong with it, was either killing it or bringing the condition to a head. This was simply a passing thought, no deep pondering or thinking.

Something else happened this year. All of our fruit in the entire orchard was stolen. We did not get one apple, we did not get one pear, we did not get one plum, and so on....from all fifty-five trees. We were not victims of human thieves, but squirrels. We had an unbelievable infestation of them during the summer months, and they stripped the trees of our fruit. Funny thing about all this. Our neighbors were blessed with an abundance of fruit, it was only our orchard that was pilfered. In retrospect, perhaps I should have realized something supernatural was taking place. Perhaps I should have realized that God might be trying to tell me something and should have taken this phenomenon to Him in prayer. I didn't.

But I certainly talked about the lost fruit, and asked neighbors and friends for any extra fruit they might have after harvest. Neighbors in our area were usually quite kind in this way, and those with an over-abundance usually shared with those who were short. But I was reduced to begging!

One day in September, my wife and I saddled our horses

and rode out on one of our summer evening rides that we treasured so much. What a thrill it is to ride out across the pasture, across the meadows, and out into the wild country. Together, we felt alone amid the natural beauty of God's world. Sometimes we ride easy, sometimes we ride hard, sometimes we talk a lot, sometimes we ride in silence. But however we go, these are precious moments, refreshing, expanding, soothing, relaxing, and stimulating.

This particular balmy evening as we sauntered past the orchard, Corinne noticed the subject pear tree was blossoming. It had set blossoms profusely all over the tree. In September! And this pear tree was the only tree in the entire orchard blossoming. We discussed how peculiar it was and I related the history of the tree to her – although she already knew it (my wife is kind to me this way, she listens to me rattle on about the same old things many times over). We discussed it only a short time and then our attentions were diverted to other things and the tree was forgotten.

About a year before this happened, I quit every job I had in our local church. I resigned from the Board of Directors, I resigned from the job of Sunday School Superintendent, and I resigned from teaching the Adult Sunday School Class. I gave as my reason that, with a new pastor coming in, I wanted him to feel free to choose whomever he wanted for those important duties. I wanted to sound generous, I wanted to sound humble, but I realized even then that I really wasn't fooling anyone, not even myself. The real reason I resigned was PRIDE. Sin. I had been hurt, and I was embittered and I could not shake it.

As the year wore on, this thing started to bother me. Not a whole lot at first, but more and more as time progressed. God has given me a gift, the gift of teaching, and I was running from it. And things started going wrong. Problems of tremendous magnitudes arose — business problems, financial problems, and family problems. Now, I am not suggesting that this plethora of problems might not have happened had I not run from God. I don't know that. But I do know that in a time-space relationship, these things all happened the year after I had quit every job I had in the church.

I had not turned my back on God. I still prayed, I still read my Bible, I still worked occasionally studying the Bible, and I had a couple of real life spiritual experiences during the year. Mini-experiences. Little lessons that the Holy Spirit taught me.

But little did I know that I was being set-up. It is always humiliating to realize that you have been set-up by another person. Imagine how much more humiliating it is to realize you have been set-up by God? And God set me up because He had something to tell me— something vitally important, something that totally crushed me.

Somewhere around the time the psychotic pear tree blossomed, I was talking on the phone one morning to the pastor. I suggested it might be advisable for the men of our tiny little mountain church to get together for an early morning prayer meeting during the week. Well, a couple of weeks later, our pastor announced from the pulpit on Sunday morning that the men of the church would have a prayer meeting the following Wednesday morning. Realizing I had triggered this, I promptly started planning ways to excuse myself from it. I tried to invent reasons, but none would jell. As I couldn't think of a way to excuse myself, I decided I would just conveniently forget it. But, when Wednesday morning came, my wife reminded me, with that tone in her voice, "You ARE going, aren't you?" I was trapped, I would have to go, no excuse not to.

In all the years I have been a Christian, many of the spiritual experiences I have had occurred when I was tired – sometimes even exhausted. And however sweet, however precious, those spiritual experiences were, doubt always crept in later. Thoughts like, "Perhaps I was just tired. Perhaps it wasn't the Holy Spirit at all, perhaps it was just my own exhausted mind and body conjuring up something I wanted." *I knew in my heart this was not so, but the doubts always plagued me. I was never sure. My faith sometimes waivered.*

Wednesday morning at 7:55AM I walked into the pastor's study – fresh, alive, and full of energy. We talked for a short time before the Chairman of the Church arrived. While the pastor handled a phone call, I told the Chairman about the squirrels stripping our orchard and asked to be remembered if his harvest was bountiful. We talked some more, about the Church, about the future of the Church, discussing options and possibilities.

Then I did something I had no intention of doing. It was the farthest thought from my mind. At least, there was no plan to do this at all. It just erupted from deep inside and I vomited out, "I have a teaching gift and I am not using it, and it is eating my guts out!" I did not mean to say that. *It was simply raw, naked truth. I had confessed before men, but really to Jesus. And Jesus heard it! I had confessed in so many words that I really wanted to be teaching again, and God knew that I was now totally set-up. He let me have it!*

We bowed our heads and the Chairman started praying. He prayed for about two or three minutes and then, out of the blue, he mentioned me, "...and Ron has had his fruit stolen..."

KAPOW!!! *God blew my mind! In one instant, quick as a wink of the eye, the Holy Spirit implanted a picture of that pear tree in my mind (I knew instantly which tree it was) and at the exact same time, He spoke to my heart and said,* ***"You're that tree."*** *That's all.*

In a flash, I saw it all. I saw the years of inedible fruit – teaching in the flesh; *and I saw no fruit at all set on this year –* quitting the job altogether. *It crushed me.*

In that instant, I fell apart emotionally and started sobbing rather uncontrollably. This, also, was not like me. There were tears of sorrow for the years of lost opportunity; there were tears of joy, tears of gratitude, and tears of thanksgiving – because the picture I saw was as it was at that time...blossoming in September!

The other fellows were not really sure what had happened, but they were aware that I had been touched. We all sat there and simply praised the Lord, thanking Him for His goodness, His tenderness, and His love.

After the prayer meeting, I went home and walked down to the orchard and stood looking at that pear tree covered with blossoms, realizing that God had set me up for years with this tree.

I am totally convinced this was the Holy Spirit. I know. There is neither question nor doubt in my mind. First, I was fresh, it was early morning. Second, I was not anticipating a spiritual experience. Third, the still, small voice came to me in the second person, i.e. "you're"... I normally think in the first person. Fourth, God in His unique way, communicated years and depths and facets of truth with one picture and three words. Fifth, Jesus, in His great love, hung hope out on the end of it with blossoms. Without them, the blow would have been too bitter. And sixth, the Holy Spirit confirmed the entire experience to my heart, which only mature Christians would understand. **Praise the Lord!**

CHAPTER NINETEEN

Twins

God Knows His Own

My son and I were on a ride one Thursday afternoon, ambling our horses toward Fire Meadow when we noticed one of our cows had a new calf. Reining in our mounts, we moved slowly toward them. Indeed, # 4 had a nice new baby. I recalled out loud that she was three or four days early, and Rick commented, " That's the smallest calf I have ever seen, and look, she has white on her ears." That remark should have been clues to me right then, and if not then, certainly later. Unfortunately, I was not sufficiently sensitive nor alert enough to recognize them.

We follow a practice of separating cows that have already calved from those still expecting. As this cow and her new calf were still in the "expecting" field, and the gate was close by, I decided to move them across right then – and we did, and thought nothing more about it.

Our next expectant mother (#5) was due the next day – Friday, but she had not delivered by Friday evening. Now, these numbers are ear-tag numbers and no significance is attached to the fact they are consecutive here. By late Saturday afternoon I was becoming a little anxious and went looking for #5. I searched for about an hour on foot in the ravines, on the hillsides, in the gullies – but I could not locate her. As I came to the top of the hill near our water-tank, I found a beautiful heifer calf. She had been licked clean and was completely dry. She was simply lying there quietly, but as I approached, she stirred and started bawling – pretty typical. I concluded that #5 had indeed calved, and this was her calf. I further concluded that #5 had gone down to the lake to get a drink and would return shortly. In the back of my mind, I suspected that something was wrong with this conclusion because mother cows rarely leave a new-born baby at least for the first twelve hours.

Nevertheless, I decided to leave the calf alone and check again about dark to see if #5 had returned.

Returning to the hilltop just as darkness was settling, I found the calf was still alone and bawling. As I stood some distance away trying to think the situation through, I witnessed a beautiful sight. The group of expectant mothers converged upon the calf. Each in her turn, sniffed the calf, and then they all formed a circle around that baby and laid down. They seemed to recognize the baby was in distress, and they all knew the baby was not theirs, but they formed this protective circle around her for the hours of darkness. It was absolutely heart touching.

I went in to have Saturday evening dinner with the family and to think more on the situation. Where was #5? Why had she not returned to her baby? And so on. I concluded during dinner that I had no choice but to go out in the dark searching again, and that I would have to stay out there until I found the calf's mother.

I bundled up heavily, took the flashlight, and went out into the night. I realized the only way I was going to find that cow was to conduct a methodical search over the whole

Fireflies

40 acre enclosure – in the dark. I had no desire to retrace any steps in the dark. (This is the same field that I had to search this way again several years later for the calf described in the chapter Let's Make a Deal)

Up the side of one hill, down the other side, through a ravine, up the side of another hill – turn, back down the hill, etc. etc. The night became still and cold, time passed, I continued to search. Temperatures dropped further and the movement of climbing and walking helped to offset the numbing chill. Up and down, back and forth, carefully – shining the light in every possible place – I continued to search.

At 11:30PM I dropped down below the upper dam and there I found #5 hidden in the brush with a beautiful new calf – still wet.

I was stunned! If this is #5's calf, to whom does that calf up on the hill belong? Could #5 have twinned? Not likely, this calf doesn't look anything like that calf up on the hill. That calf up there is small and *has white on its ears*......oh, oh, wait a minute....the truth hit me like a thunderbolt! **Number 4** – the cow we had moved to the other pasture last Thursday. I had forgotten #4 had a history of occasionally twinning. She must have twinned again and forgotten this calf. And I had insured that she would forget it, by moving her to another pasture!

I raced back up the hill to the house. Breathless, I roused Corinne and asked her to help me. I told her I knew whose calf that was up there, and that poor baby has had no nourishment for three days — the first three days of her life!

We drove the truck up the hill to the water tank, and approached the herd on foot in the lights of the truck. The little thing was still all alone in the center of the circle, surrounded by the expectant mothers. Picking her up gently in my arms, I carried her to the truck and put her in the bed of the truck with Corinne. We had to drive about a half-mile to the area where the herd of mothers and babies were. They also sort of congregate at night. Down and around the hill we drove, past the barn, past the orchard, around the lower lake, across the dam, around another hill and out across the meadow. We found the herd and I managed to put the headlights on #4 cow who was standing with her calf. Almost exactly at midnight, I stopped the truck about 50 yards from her, walked to the back, and picked up the calf again in my arms. I started walking toward #4.

When #4 saw me approaching in the headlight beams, she lowed softly to her calf beside her – calling the calf to safety, to remain by her side. But an incredible thing happened! The calf in my arms recognized that little lowing call **as her own mother**! She responded immediately with an urgent bawl of her own and commenced struggling fiercely to get out of my arms!

As the calf in my arms started bawling and struggling, #4 cow reacted like she had been given an electric shock! She jumped, came instantly alert, looked at the calf by her side, looked back at us, and became very excited and confused. She recognized the calf in my arms as her own, but knew she already had one!

About 15 yards from the cow, I could no longer hold the struggling, active calf. I put her down and she ran directly to her mother. The calf wanted to suck, she was starved, but the mother did not want her to suck – she wanted to smell her. Round and around they went, with the cow not letting her suck – and the poor baby was famished. The cow kept going from one calf to the other, sniffing and smelling, cooing and lowing, but kept turning in circles, denying any access to her faucets.

Finally, we decided there was nothing more for us to do until morning. We said a little prayer for them, wished them well, and headed off to bed. I realized that if they were still turning in circles in the morning, the trio would have to be put in the corral, run into the chute, and care taken of the situation.

At first light on Sunday morning, I got Rick out of bed, and we headed down to the barn. We saddled the horses and rode out to the herd. Rounding the last bend, we cleared the last tree just as the sun came peeking over the hill. Then, we beheld an absolutely beautiful sight in the morning solitude. Number 4 was standing placidly chewing her cud, while both little twins – one on each side – were nursing her with their tails wagging.

Recognition of the relationship between the mother and the baby came upon receiving the communication. The communication was physical and audible.

But what about communication between God and man? The question is not 'does it exist,' but **how** *does it exist? Especially from God to man. There is a lot of confusion about this. I tend to think one of the reasons for the confusion is that God deals with different people in different ways, and with the same person in different ways at different times. Perhaps I am assuming, but I believe the Bible teaches that all communication from God to man is made by the Holy Spirit.*

The following categorical summary is no attempt to either defend or debunk the claims and methods by which various Christians have testified that God has spoken to them. It is not the purpose here to challenge the veracity of any Christian, but to set forth the various methods. These break into three natural categories: (1) Supernatural experience; (2) Audible; and (3) Inaudible.

Supernatural ways *include dreams, visions, and out-of-body experiences. Some people witness to these upon their conversion, like the Apostle Paul. Others claim to experience them somewhat regularly and frequently. A few people claim to have had one or two such experiences in their lifetime. But by far, the vast majority has never experienced* these at all. I believe we might hear more of this as time goes on. The prophet Joel wrote,

> **"And afterward, I will pour out my Spirit on all people; Your sons and daughters will prophesy, your old men will dream dreams, your young men will see visions."** Joel 2:28

Audible. A few people claim to have heard the audible voice of the Holy Spirit in their ears. I have never experienced this, so cannot comment upon it one way or another.

Also in the audible area, but quite different from hearing the voice of God are prophecies and tongues-with-interpretations which come from the mouths of men. These are well known in Pentecostal and Charismatic circles and usually are not directed to an individual but to a body of people. Many of them are delivered in the first person as God would speak – but nevertheless, the sound is being made by a human being.

Inaudible. Most people who claim to have heard God's voice will tell you it was not audible, but spiritual. They can only describe it as I have done in the chapters on "Let's Make A Deal," "The Mower," and "The Pear Tree." It is a still, small voice speaking directly to the spirit. Now some people claim to have carried on whole conversations with God in this manner. Others, like my own experience, say God speaks to them in a single word, or at most – a very few words – which carry incredible depths of meaning, often accompanied with a significant vision, as described in the Pear Tree chapter.

Whether or not any Christian has received communications from God, be it supernaturally, audibly, or inaudibly as described above, every Christian has received direct communication from the Spirit of God. It is the Spirit of God, the Holy Spirit, who is tugging at your heart, calling *you, urging you to respond to the gospel message of salvation in the first place. Then, upon accepting Jesus Christ as your personal savior, it is the Holy Spirit who 'confirms' your faith, giving you assurance of salvation. Isn't it true that every 'true' Christian* **knows** *he has eternal life? He isn't 'hoping' he will go to heaven, he knows he will be going to heaven. These are important communications. Don't be concerned if God has never spoken to you with some personal message. Just rejoice that He has called you to salvation, and communicated His love and joy, and peace to your heart.*

Prayer. *Communication from man to God. It can be either audible or inaudible, as God knows the heart. A very good case can be made for recommending audible prayer, however. It tends to keep the person praying progressing in logical fashion. Short, silent prayers are alright, but long, involved, silent prayers often lead to thought distraction, mind wandering, and even sleep.*

The language of prayer.

Many Christians make it a point to speak to God in a special language, a language that they inwardly feel (but don't want to outwardly admit) that God perhaps will listen a little more intently. They feel God will be more likely to honor their petitions because this 'holy' language shows their awe and respect for Him. We touched on this briefly in our chapter on Boysenberries.

Frankly, all of this is nonsense. The language is called Old English – the language that the King James translation of the Bible was published in some 400 years ago. So, people pray to God using "thee" and "thy" and "thou," and words like doth, hath, wouldest, shouldest, and so on thinking they are being reverent.

God doesn't care about that! God is not interested in form, He is interested in substance. God is not impressed with archaic words, He is reading the heart. God is not influenced by flowery phrases as much as He is with sincere praises! God's stethoscope is more important than His ears. That is to say, God is more interested in what He hears from your heart than from your mouth. Don't expect God to honor a prayer because you use a language no longer spoken nor generally used, He is impressed with honesty, humility, and yielding to His will.

More about language

Jesus spoke in Aramaic as far as we know. That was the common language of the day. There is Biblical evidence that when He prayed and talked to His Father, He spoke in Aramaic – Mark 15:34 and Matt. 27:46. On the other hand, the Old Testament was written in ancient Hebrew, another language altogether. Jesus certainly quoted the OT from time to time, but did not speak or address crowds in that language.

Furthermore, the New Testament was originally written in common, everyday-spoken Greek, called the Koine, not the classical Greek of Homer. Those two languages are about as far apart as our modern English is with the King James English.

Parenthetically, think about these two facts for a minute. Jesus spoke in one language, and the writers of the gospels recorded him in another. How else could this have happened had the Holy Spirit not guided the writers? This is indeed remarkable.

Is it not reasonable then, that we should address our God in our everyday language? Is the use of the Old English more pious? Is the use of the Old English more respectful?

Use of the Old English does have one effect, though, **a negative one**. It really turns off the potential converts of the younger generation who are so sensitive to hypocrisy, false piousness, and pompous self-righteousness. It becomes a *giant stumbling block to those who "almost believe" but just want to be themselves. They are afraid that if they become Christians, they will have to learn this new language and talk with "thee, thou, and thy." And so on, and it all sounds so phony to them.*

So, there seems to be no positive reasons for the Old English, only negative ones. Why use it at all? Why not communicate with God just as we are, just as we talk, instead of trying to be something we are not?

CHAPTER TWENTY

The Day the Lamb Died

The life is in the blood!

The story of Dividend's birth was related in an earlier chapter. Remember? He was born of a "sterile" ewe sheep, and we learned that God indeed hears our prayers and rewards our faith – *but in His own time and in His own way*. Dividend came to us as a reward of Corinne's faith.

"Divie" was a cute little fellow. As he grew up, he loved to run and jump for the sheer joy of being alive. I have noticed that both calves and lambs particularly enjoy racing about in nonsense play around dusk each evening. Divie was no exception. He would bolt out of the stall and down the pen as fast as he could run. Then he would slam on the brakes just before he hit the fence, pause an instant – then jump right up in the air with all four legs stiffened, turn and race back to his mother. Back and forth, this went on for about an hour each evening.

But there came a time when he had to be weaned and fattened for the freezer. We were careful not to make a pet out of him lest we become too emotionally attached.

Inevitably, his "time" came.

Now Divie was a perfect lamb in the sense he was without blemish. He was neither lame nor sick, but was sound and in good health. However, Divie had a large brown spot on his back. If I interpret the Bible correctly, he would not have been eligible for sacrifice had he been born in Old Testament Israel. First Peter 1:19 clarifies by making a distinction between blemish and spot. The verse infers that both were unacceptable. Anyway, it is unimportant as far as this lesson goes.

The day of his slaughter arrived. Two men entered his enclosure and tried to catch him. He wanted no part of it, bolting and racing and jumping – continually eluding his captors.

I thought of Jesus. His cousin, John, when he saw Jesus coming, said, **"Look, the Lamb of God who takes away the sin of the world."** *John 1:29. Jesus was God's lamb – without spot or blemish. He was perfect in every way – physically, mentally, emotionally, spiritually – sinless!*

And Jesus eluded His captors. There are at least six different occasions recorded in the Gospel of John where Jesus slipped away from those who tried to capture Him. (6:15; 7:1; 7:30; 7:44; 8:59; 10:39)

Eventually, the little lamb Divie was caught. After all the running and eluding, he finally just stopped and stood still. He simply gave up and allowed the men to grab him.

Eventually Jesus was caught. When He decided or knew the time was right, He simply stood still, allowing the soldiers to capture Him.

The men threw the lamb on the ground, a knife flashed, and Divie's blood gushed!

From His hands and His feet, Jesus' blood oozed and flowed – down the inside of His arm, into His armpit, on down His side – clear to the end of His feet where it trickled to the ground. But when the soldier stepped up and hurled the spear into His side, Jesus' blood gushed! The blood of God!

The biological sciences established many years ago the fact that an individual's blood is derived from or is determined by the father. They also established that maternal blood and fetal blood never mix. There is no common exchange of blood between a mother and her baby during gestation — no co-mingling. Jesus blood never mixed with Mary's. Food and nourishment are transferred from the mother's blood to the baby by capillary action and an absorption process called osmosis. Their bloods do not mix, they are separate, individual, and unique. Occasionally, they are of different types and characteristics.

Mary was impregnated by the Holy Spirit! Therefore, the blood in **Jesus veins was God's blood!** Luke 1:31-35

Jesus was the lamb of God, perfect in every respect, worthy to be offered in sacrifice to God for the sins of the world. The sacrifice was accomplished by shedding Jesus' blood.

Zombi

A zombi is a voodoo concept of living death. It is a mythical person whose body is dead, yet it moves and functions and animates – without any blood. A zombi is bloodless, living death!

Many cults in the world build their religious order or system on Jesus Christ. Many of them have the name Jesus Christ or Christian in their own name. Some of them teach that Jesus was not God, but a mere man to be emulated. Others of them think of Him not as a man, but only God who came to teach us his principles. And so on they go. But all of them – universally – deny the necessity of Jesus' blood for salvation. The idea of shedding blood, to them, is an unnecessary, unfortunate, repulsive, primitive concept. I rather think that they classify themselves as zombis – bloodless, living death!

No Christianity without Blood

Blood is splashed across the entire Bible! There is no Christianity whatsoever without Jesus blood! There is no salvation, no justification, no propitiation, no redemption, no sanctification, no overcoming, —- nothing!

Let's just list here how the Bible makes the necessity of Jesus blood patently clear:

TYPE: *"For the life of a creature is in the blood: and I have given it to you to make an atonement for yourselves on the altar souls: it is the blood that makes atonement for one's life." Leviticus 17:11*

NECESSITY: *"Without the shedding of blood there is no forgiveness." Hebrews 9:22*

PRICE: *"...be shepherds of the church of God which he bought with his own blood." Acts 20:28*

PURIFIES: *"...and the blood of Jesus. His Son purifies us from all sin." I John 1:7*

JUSTIFIES: *"Since we have now been justified by his blood..." Romans 5:9*

PEACE WITH GOD: *"...by making peace through the blood, shed on the cross... Col. 1:20*

OVERCOMING: *"...They overcame him (Satan) by the blood of the lamb." Revelation 12:11*

Fireflies

One last observation. The lamb, Divie, did not struggle! He simply laid there and bled to death. Obediently. Without fuss, without fight – he resigned himself to his fate.

Jesus did the same thing for you. When His time came, He was obedient. He simply hung there and bled to death. He even asked His Father to forgive those who crucified Him. He gave up His life for you – so you might live forever – with Him. Peter called Jesus' blood "precious." God's blood. It was able to cover the sin of the entire world. It was shed for you and me, each and every person who has ever lived.

Wonderful Thought!

The pastor at our church proposed an interesting thought I wish to pass along to you. He said that the first thing he wants to do when he meets Jesus face to face is to fall down on his knees and thank Jesus for dying for him. What a magnificent thought!

All Jesus asks of you is to believe in Him – put your faith and trust in Him – in His blood. He'll do the rest.

How will you respond?

CHAPTER TWENTY-ONE

The Heifer Kicked

Rejection!

A little surprise greeted me the other afternoon as I entered the feedlot to dispense the evening feeding to the cattle. (To keep nutrition levels up during the early spring, we feed a little hay until the grass is up and strong enough to do the job). As I was a bit early, the cattle had not yet come in, but there in the middle of the feedlot was a brand new baby calf. Not only was he new, but he had not been licked clean. He was simply lying there, blinking, covered with all the slime associated with birth. Most of it had dried, so he had probably been born much earlier in the day. His mother was nowhere in sight.

The cows soon came in for their dinner and it was not difficult to determine which heifer was the new mother. She was separated and put into a small corral with her calf. The calf was eager to feed, but the mother wanted no part of it. When the little bull baby approached her, she would butt him with her head, and keep on butting him, knocking him right off his feet. However, he was a determined little guy, and he would get right up and try again. When he did manage to get near those faucets for a meal, the heifer would kick at him viciously.

There surely didn't appear to be much maternal instinct in this heifer. In addition, another thing was absent. Usually mamas talk to their calves, with continued soft, short, lowing sounds, but this heifer had nothing to say to her baby. On the contrary, he annoyed her, made her nervous, and she continually kept trying to get away from him. One might conclude that we had the wrong heifer, but we made absolutely certain this was her calf.

In times past we have had success in immobilizing the cow in the steel squeeze and then giving the calf a chance to suck. If you remember, this was the procedure with Howie in an earlier chapter, so we tried this. What an ordeal this one turned out to be. The heifer kicked herself into a frenzy, and finally we had to tie her legs back so her baby could get his first meal. I was suspicious at this point that she was not going to take him, but we locked them in together and did all the right things and left them.

It was the same story at midnight. Every time the calf would get near his mother, she would strike out at him with her hoof, kicking him halfway across the corral. She simply did not want her son. She was rejecting her son.

The questions and decisions facing me were these. Was this heifer ultimately going to take her son and love him and nurture him? Or was she going to continue rejecting him thereafter? And, how long should she be allowed to kick him until a decision is made?

And the decision was all mine!

Finally, the decision was made. Separate them. **Forever.** The calf was picked up and brought up to the barn where he was hand-fed, and the heifer was turned out.

There is an old saying among cattlemen: Never give a cow a second chance! This is the principle of culling. If a cow makes a mistake and does not raise a calf, ship her to slaughter. I have violated that axiom on three different occasions in years past and have regretted it each time. Three times I have given cows a second chance, and three times they repeated their mistakes once again. You might think I am a slow learner — perhaps so — or maybe simply too forgiving, or optimistic — whatever.

And it would have been easy to seduce me into giving this heifer another chance. She had everything going for her. She was of excellent genetic, hereditary lines; she had outstanding conformation; and was generally a superior individual. But she rejected her son. And the moment the decision was made to separate them forever, this heifer's number went on the shipping list. This heifer would be included in the next shipment to the slaughterhouse. Although she was turned out to pasture and had total freedom with the other cattle for the time being, she was already dead!

But, as her master, I did not seal her doom – she did! She rejected her son. Had she shown any signs of interest, had she talked to the calf, had she been curious, or drawn to him in any way to signify she felt guilt or responsibility, she would have been given more time, more opportunity to accept him. But she did not. She just wanted to get away from him.

She got her wish.

God's lesson is so plainly evident. There is one sin Jesus did not die for – rejection of Him! If a person rejects the Son of God, indeed, kicks at Him, there will come a time when the Master makes the decision to remove all further opportunity.

Crossing the Line

Where is the line? At what point does a person ultimately lose all chance to accept the Son of God?

Physical death is the ultimate point. No one in this

world has any assurance of physical life from moment to moment. Physical death and destruction can overtake any human being at any time by accidents, crime, failure of the body systems, or any number of things.

But even those folks who experience a long life-time are often overtaken in mental death in their old age. They reach a point where the mind becomes senile and cannot operate on a comprehending level. They reach a point where they cannot accept the Son of God and be born again because they cannot comprehend. The mysterious crossing the line, then, for them was somewhere before physical death.

Spiritually, any one who has not been born again, **is already dead**! They have no spiritual life whatsoever. They have no chance at all until and unless they accept the Son of God, Jesus Christ, as their personal Savior. Personal. Their own. Their names are already on the list to go to the slaughterhouse – hell! They might live on for a spell, any number of years, but their ultimate disposition is DEATH! What a tragedy!

What about the person who accepts Jesus Christ as his Savior and subsequently rejects Him? Your author is no theologian and has no desire to fan the fire of this great controversy. The question is: Can Faith, once established, subsequently and ultimately reject Grace?

This question recalls one of the three cows I mentioned earlier as having given them a second chance. The particular cow in mind was #16. She gave birth to a nice calf when she was a first time heifer. They were kept in a small, enclosed field for three days and she stood for the calf to nurse and gave all the appearances of being a good mother. After three days, they were turned out. The second night they were out, a terrible blizzard visited our area. The following morning I found the cow #16, but not the calf. A full- scale search for the calf resulted in finding his body a few hours later nestled up next to a log. We were not sure why the calf died. Had he died from exposure to the severe elements? Did the calf die because he had not been fed in addition to the exposure? What exactly had happened? I did not know. I decided to give #16 another chance and breed her again.

The following year she was in the same enclosed field to calve, and deliberately left in there with her calf for over a week after the event. All seemed to be going well, so they were turned out into our distant pasture. Unfortunately, I got busy and was unable to check on him for about five days, although I felt I had no reason to worry about him. How wrong I was. When I found him, he was already dead. We happened to have a truck going to the slaughterhouse the next day, and #16 became a last minute passenger!

Number #16 accepted her son, walked with him, and lived with him for a spell, but ultimately rejected him. She savored her freedom more than her responsibility. Her first love was herself. Her selfish ways seemed right to her, but they were the ways of death. Her death.

But, can a person be born again, accept Jesus Christ, and walk for a while with Him, then reject Him? And if so, where is the mysterious "line" that is crossed that makes the rejection ultimate? Where is there no more chance to repent?

The only answer can be: the Master decides. For some it might be physical death. For others, it might be some point before physical death – a point where God decides no more opportunity will be given. The person is already dead, then, at that point. It has been suggested that when this latter occurs, that person will not care. Either mental death or permanent hardness of the heart will have occurred.

If this frightens you, if this bothers you, if this upsets you, then your heart has not been permanently hardened. God is still dealing with you. God is still calling you to repent. God is quoted in the Old Testament,

> *"If my people, who are called by my name, will humble themselves and pray and seek My face and turn from their wicked ways, then I will hear from heaven, and will forgive their sin...."* II Chronicles 7:14

But God has gone on further to say in the New Testament in II Peter 2:20-21

> *"If they have escaped the corruption of the world by knowing our Lord and Savior Jesus Christ and are again entangled in it and overcome, they are worse off at the end than they were at the beginning. It would have been better for them not to have known the way of righteousness than to have known it and then to turn their backs on the sacred command that was passed on to them."*

If the first state is spiritual death, what is the last state that can be worse? Would that be spiritual death with the knowledge in eternal consciousness of once having had eternal life and willfully rejecting it?

And we find further in Revelation 3:5 **"He who overcomes...I will never blot out his name from the book of life..."** Does this not imply that some names can and will be blotted out?

Are you kicking at Jesus now? Kicking is indeed an apt description. As the heifer kicked at her calf, so men and women kick at Jesus. I Samuel 2:29 and Acts 9:4 (in the King James Version) give examples of kicking – an act of disrespect, contempt, and rejection. How long will you continue to kick?

CHAPTER TWENTY TWO

Apples, Apples, Apples

Myth dispelled!

Corinne and I own and operate Stout's Cider Mill on Interstate 10 in Arizona. When we relocated to southeastern Arizona, planting apple orchards was in vogue. We were among the many farming folks who collectively planted over 5,000 acres and over a million trees in the area. We personally planted over 10,000 trees initially, and at the peak of our production had over 25,000 trees before downsizing our operation.

There are many aspects to this fruit that can yield interesting analogies to Biblical lessons. In modern apple production, the selection of varieties, the methods of growing and delivering water, the choice and use of protection pesticides, techniques of harvest, and storage technologies are all among the areas where definite options exist. In most cases here, once decisions are made, the farmer is 'locked in' to that decision for years to come.

Why apples? The U.S. Apple Association makes the case on their website that an apple is a highly nutritious fruit. Consider, if you will, that this fruit is fat free; saturated fat free; sodium free; cholesterol free; and also an important source of fiber. In addition, apples are an outstanding source of boron, plant anti-oxidants, and contain natural fruit sugars. Their high fiber content causes the natural sugars to be released into the blood stream slowly, thus maintaining blood sugar levels. The classic old saying, "*An apple a day keeps the doctor away,*" has a lot of truth in it. Actually, that saying is derived from a centuries old English saying paraphrased here, "*Eat an apple before going to bed; Makes the doctor beg his bread.*"

Why did we choose apples? First, apples requiring a long growing season were found to thrive in the American Southwest. Second, methods of storing apples for long periods of time were developed to facilitate a year-round business.

Every year at harvest, we initially store apples in half-ton bins and then after sorting they are packed into cardboard cartons or boxes. These are placed in regular commercial refrigerators from harvest time until the following summer. That is a long time to keep a fresh apple *without* some kind of oxygen deprivation storage. We do it simply out of necessity. We are not privileged to own Controlled Atmosphere storage. This latter figuratively 'puts the fruit to sleep' and allows it to rest unchanged until oxygen is introduced again. The presence of oxygen near and around the fruit causes the fruit to mature and ripen and continues the process to spoilage. This is a function of time. When a fruit is bruised, the process is hastened.

If we have to buy fruit 'off-season,' we usually buy fruit that has been kept in CA storage and transfer it to our own commercially refrigerated, cold storage units. When we sort and size our fruit in the Fall, we are careful not to bruise the fruit, nor pass already bruised fruit into the storage boxes.

"*One rotten apple in the barrel spoils the whole*

thing." This saying has evolved from its beginnings way back in the days of Chaucer. At that time, Chaucer said, "***The rotten apple injures its neighbors***." A somewhat different concept, but nevertheless, the idea is there.

Guess what! I have a secret.

I have discovered that today's saying is not true! Really — not true! Let me explain what we have found. After the fruit has been in regular commercial refrigerated storage for a long time, like 9-10 months, almost all of the fruit has deteriorated to a brown, spoiled, fermented mush. In a word, it is **rotten.** But we have found a very curious thing! If we stick our arms down into that rotten mess, we can discover a few **absolutely perfect apples** that have been totally submerged, in direct contact with mushy, rotten ones! When washed and cleaned up, they make marvelous juice! In a 40 pound box of apples, we often can salvage up to 3-4 pounds of these. Now, this is not a practice we engage in regularly. Obviously, it could not be cost effective to do this, nor make any sense. But in the 'dog days' of summer, before harvest, we sometimes must resort to this for juice apples. I regard these apples as special! They have resided in and among rots for weeks on end and have not been tainted!

Horse Racing

When I was almost six years old, my mother went into the hospital for the birth of my one and only sibling. This was in the latter part of September, coincident with the two-week Los Angeles County Fair at Pomona, California.

Now my grandfather Stout owned and trained thoroughbred race-horses and had his stable at the Pomona Fair. My Dad, Lex, took his vacation at that time, so Lex and Ronnie went to the fair. I slept in a straw covered stall each night with horses in the stalls on either side. I absolutely fell in love with racing. I was captivated by the excitement at the track, the electricity of the crowds, the staccato tones of the bugle, the majestic prancing horses drawing the red wagon up the track in between races, and the tailored and manicured infield and track. To a six year old, it was simply awe inspiring.

I watched carefully as my grandfather would stand off to the side and observe 'our horse' as the groom walked him into the saddling paddock. Granddad would approach the horse, take hold of his halter and speak softly and gently to the animal. After petting his head, he would run his hands slowly down over the front legs, satisfying himself the horse was sound enough to run.

The saddle blanket with the race number was put on the horse's back and adjusted into place while the bridle was slipped into the mouth. Then the little patch of leather called a saddle was tossed up there, adjusted and cinched tight. The riders appeared from a doorway and walked to the horses. Our rider would be wearing white silks with a red English "S" on his back and a red cap with goggles pushed up over the bill. His black, shiny boots sparkled in the sunlight as he walked toward us with a self-confident swagger carrying his riding crop. Standing there near my grandfather, I listened to the racing instructions, and was thrilled by the glamour of it all. *That is what I wanted to be in life* – **a jockey**. That would bring many laughs in our extended family (actually guffaws from the older men) as I was already almost too big and too heavy at 6 years old for that profession.

The call "Rider's Up" would come. Granddad would reach down, grab his jockey's leg and hoist him high into the air onto the back of the horse. The last thing granddad would do was to slap the jockey on the leg, and drop a "win" ticket into his boot. Horse and rider, the jockey's silks fluttering in the breeze, would be led into the tunnel under the grandstand, as the sounds of the bugle called the horses to the track. Those activities were the 'front end' of the track.

The backstretch or 'back-end' was a different story. The men who worked the stables in those days, circa 1936, were often unstable. They had long ago succumbed to and were shackled to many unclean habits. Probably the worst one was swearing. Many of these men could not speak even one complete sentence without including profanity and vulgarity.

Now these horses are high-strung animals, and they kick, knock over their feed buckets, and are often cantankerous. You can imagine the cesspool of swearing heard constantly around the stables, in a word – **rotten.** In that period I stayed at the track, I was exposed to it. I heard it. I was too young to understand much of it, but I knew it was evil.

A few years later, but in that same era, something happened that I have always wondered about. An elderly couple started attending our church and the gentleman responded and accepted Jesus Christ as his personal Savior. He had a wonderful testimony and exuded the love of Jesus. It turned out that this man was a regular farrier at the southern California tracks.

Conflict developed in the church. The minister insisted the man quit his job and leave the track. However, shoeing horses was the only job this elderly gentleman knew, and it was the only job he was qualified and trained to do. The reason given was that "it was not the place for Christians." On the other hand, some felt that Jesus knew where this man worked. Jesus loved him and saved him, certainly Jesus would be able to keep him. Furthermore, many felt that Jesus wanted this man to be a witness 'on the backstretch.' Unfortunately, I do not remember how this situation resolved itself, and I am afraid there is no one alive today who accurately remembers at this distance in time.

The principle here is gigantic. Does Jesus want us to separate ourselves from the world, live in our own little, closed society of Christian believers? Enter a monastery? If He does, how then can we possibly be *"...**the salt of the*** *earth?"* Matthew 5:13. In order for salt to work, it must be spread out, around, and over the food. *Doesn't it make more sense for Jesus to want us simply to witness for Him, and to live our Christian life in the* **setting we have been placed?**

I have not thought of this man or this situation for over sixty years. Why was it that when I reached down in that box of rotten apples, fished around in the mush, pulled out a pristine, whole apple, and looked at it in amazement, that the farrier came to mind?

In closing, this apple thought for the day is offered. It was found on the internet, and attributed to folklore:

> **"Anyone can count the number of seeds in an apple, but only God can count the number of apples in a seed."**

CHAPTER TWENTY THREE

The Door is Open

Nothing happens until it is!

Our first little ranch was in the mountains of Southern California just above the 4,000 foot altitude. Our climate was not as mild as that of the coastal plain in which Los Angeles and San Diego lie. Nevertheless, there were a number of years where precipitation had been far below normal all over the state. As a matter of fact, California was declared a drought area after several such years in succession. Water shortages were having their effect in many cities and communities all over the state.

Now most of California's rainfall is experienced in the winter. Just the opposite is true of southeastern Arizona, where the summer monsoons bring most of the annual rainfall. The winter droughts in California result from immobile, stationary high-pressure cells sitting off the Pacific Coast. This static high-pressure acted as a door – shutting out those storms that formed in the Gulf of Alaska and normally headed our way. The new storms would form up there and work their way down the Pacific Coast until they would run into the 'door,' causing them to turn eastward across Washington and Oregon into other western states. Meanwhile, we would sit under warm, sunny skies with no rain, no snow, no moisture to speak of – resulting in very little grass, a dangerous lowering of the water table, and extreme fire hazard conditions all summer.

The approaching winter looked like it was going to be repeat of this condition that had prevailed for several years. By Thanksgiving, there had been no rainfall, the weather was balmy, and we actually ate Thanksgiving dinner outside in short-sleeve shirts. There was no change in this condition until shortly before Christmas.

One week before Christmas I stood outside the barn, reflecting on the moisture situation that seemed hopeless. I kicked the dirt and the dust flew. It indeed seemed like it would never rain again. The fields and meadows had no grass at all, just lying there in their barrenness. The lakes were as low as I had ever seen them, and all the springs had long since dried up. Many diverse thoughts can run through a person's mind as he tries to reason and cope with a problem of this magnitude, i.e. so big he cannot act, can only react.

This is not an account of great faith. This is not a story of beseeching God on our behalf for rain. We did, in fact, mention rain to Him, but honestly it was more an addendum to our daily prayers. "Oh, yes, Lord, we would thank you for some rain."— really not anything more than that.

That very evening, the evening of the day I stood and kicked the dirt, the newscaster made an announcement that I shall never forget. The barometer was falling, and the weatherman said, "Ladies and gentlemen, I have some good news for you this evening. The high pressure that has been sitting off our coast for so long has finally moved eastward over the Rockies, leaving an open path for the storms developing up near Alaska to descend directly upon us. *The door is open*, and we expect rainfall."

Indeed, the door was open. Before morning we heard the drip, drip, drip of water coming off the roof. The rain had started!

And the storms came, one after another, some riding right on the heels of the preceding storm, some pausing a few days, but in rapid succession through December. And they kept coming, through January, through February, it continued to storm. We received more than a double portion during that period. It was marvelous. The lakes filled, the fields turned from brown to green, the water table rose. Oh, it was not all good, there were some hardships. Areas flooded, bridges washed out, more than one person lost their lives in the San Diego area. We lost a prize show calf who got stuck in a bog.

Earlier I said this was not a story of great faith. By the same token, it is not an attempt to reason the fathomless depth of God's intelligence by trying to discover "why" we had no rain for so long, and "why" we got so much in such a short period. Nor is this an attempt to moralize or rationalize concerning the loss of life and property damage caused by the storms.

No, this whole chapter has only to do with the cause and effect relationship. The rain did not come because the door was shut. As soon as the door was open, the rain came and the storms continued one after another.

Jesus said, "Here I am! I stand at the door and knock: if anyone hears my voice, and opens the door, I will come in and eat with him, and he with me." Revelation 3:20

The doors of men's hearts are closed. Jesus is shut out. There can be no blessings, no fellowship, no rewards, as long as the doors are closed. But Jesus is still out there knocking and speaking. Perhaps to you, right at this very moment. He loves you and wants to commune with you.

Now here is the really good part. You don't have to do anything to be "worthy" of this invitation. I have heard people say that you have to "give" your heart to Jesus. Frankly, I can't find where the Bible teaches that. What's wrong with the concept of "giving your heart to Jesus?" Plenty. First, <u>give</u> implies a gift. Now, a gift is usually something of value, something to be treasured, something nice, something presented with pride. That last word alone should be a red flag.

> **"The heart is deceitful above all things and beyond cure. Who can understand it?"**
> Jeremiah 17:9

Logically progressing, if you are going to "give" something to Jesus that is wicked and unclean, then by all means, you ought to clean it up before giving it. You need to live a good life, to not sin, and prepare your heart to give to Jesus. Right? Wrong! It cannot be done, it is impossible.

In fact, I believe the Bible teaches just the opposite!

> **"Yet to all who received him, to those who believed in his name, he gave the right to become the sons of God." John 1:12**

<u>Receive</u> is just the opposite of <u>give</u>, isn't it? Exactly! All that is required is that you believe that Jesus died for your sins—yours, personally – and that He arose from the dead and lives today. Then honestly and sincerely **open the door of your heart**, asking Him to come in and save you to eternal life. Receive Him.

He will come into your heart, and you will know true happiness, true joy, true love as the blessings of Christ pour into your life from above.

CHAPTER TWENTY FOUR

Harvest

The work to be done

Our garden consumes a great amount of time and labor. Two times during the year activity is at its greatest – planting time and harvest time. Of the two, the harvest is by far the greatest task. Quantities sufficient to last the family for an entire year are brought in for storage, processing, and preserving. Many hands are required in the late summer-early fall race against the coming winter freeze. Sometimes those hands are the same ones who did the planting months earlier, but more often than not on our farm, the harvesters are not the original planters.

Most of the harvesting is done by hand. However, there are some commodities that cannot be gathered by hand, an implement or tool must be used. The potato is a good example. When the potato is mature, its plant above the ground dries out and dies. It can receive no more nourishment from the sunlight above. The dried plant often breaks off and occasionally even disappears. A fork or shovel is necessary to dig deep into the earth to uncover and dislodge the potatoes. (And no matter how thorough we think we have been in harvesting these tubers, we always discover the following spring that some have been missed when potatoes "volunteer" in last year's patch.)

Spiritual Blindness

In reflecting upon the reasons why people reject Christianity, I have come to realize that many people cannot be reached by man alone. Jesus said, " I am the Light of the world." As the potato has eyes but cannot see, so do many people have spiritual eyes but cannot see because they are in the depths of darkness like the potato. All contact with the Light of the world has withered and died.

> **"And even if our gospel is veiled, it is veiled to those that are perishing: The god of this age has blinded the minds of unbelievers so that they cannot see the light of the gospel of the glory of Christ, who is the image of God."** *II Corinthians 4:3-4*

Now the god of this world, as mentioned above, is not our Lord Jesus Christ, but Satan himself, as established in various places in the gospel of John. Satan has blinded the eyes of those who do not believe. These people invariably believe there is no God and that everything has happened by chance. They believe evolution is the answer to the happenings in the universe. They cannot reconcile events in life and believe there is no life after death. They are atheists. They are spiritually blind.

The implement or the power to expose them to the Light is none other than God Himself. God must peel away the darkness from their spiritual eyes that they may see the Light and see the Way. But there is something here that we should not miss.

As the fork, or shovel, that uncovers the potatoes is directed and operated by man, so is the power that allows God to implant sight in blind spiritual eyes directed and motivated by man. It is called prayer. God's plan is for people to win other people for Jesus Christ. When this cannot be done directly, then prayer is the only avenue available for it to be accomplished.

"Take your sickle and reap, because the time to reap has come; for the harvest of the earth is ripe." Revelation 14:15

Other examples of produce that require a tool for harvest are the small grains: wheat, oats, barley, and others. A sharp knife, attached to a wooden handle, is used to cut down the stalks. There are two hand tools for this operation: the sickle and the scythe.

The sickle is a small, single-handed tool with a curved blade, while the scythe is a large, two-handed tool with a long handle. They both do the same work. Their difference is in how they are used and the amount of work that can be accomplished. In the modern world, mechanized equipment has been designed to harvest grains, but the machines basically do the same job as the scythe. They cut the stalks of grain and send them on to the thresher. Much of the world still uses the hand scythe. Great quantities of grain stalks are out cut down, gathered and bunched, and transported to the threshing floor to separate the grain from the stalk.

This harvesting operation is a vivid picture of the evangelist or preacher. His tool is the sharp Sword of the Spirit – the Bible.

"For the word of God is living and active. Sharper than any double-edged sword, it penetrates even to dividing of soul and

spirit, joints and marrow; it judges the thoughts and attitudes of the heart."
Hebrews 4:12

Skillfully using the word of God, the evangelist goes through the fields, cutting a swath and gathering bunches for Christ. Whether he uses the platform or the electronic media, the difference is only in the amount of work accomplished.

One by One

All other fruits from our orchard and garden are harvested individually by hand. But the methods vary: some are picked up, some are pulled out, some are picked off, some are cut off, and others are broken loose.

Picking up the harvest off the ground is stoop labor. Melons, squash, pumpkins, and nuts are in this category. Of course, the nuts have fallen off the tree, whereas the melons develop and ripen on the ground. Cantaloupes are interesting. When they ripen, their attaching vine withers and dies right at the point of connection with the fruit., letting the harvester know the melon is ripe.

Pulling vegetables **out** of the ground is another method of harvest. Carrots, beets, radishes, turnips, onions, leeks, and others are representative of this group. Here again, the method is stoop labor, usually giving way to being down on one's hands and knees after awhile.

Picking off is the harvest method most frequently used. Most orchard fruits, grapes, berries, tomatoes, peppers, beans, and many others are separated from their source in this manner. The easiest picking, of course, is when the laborer works in a comfort level where he neither has to stoop nor stretch. Great quantities can be gathered at one time picking in baskets or boxes for transport to the barn or the house.

Cutting off the produce is another method. Asparagus, cabbage, lettuce, and others are treated this way. True, a small knife is required, but the vegetables are harvested individually, one at a time.

Snapping off is the most efficient way to harvest corn, brussel sprouts and "snap" beans. The ears or heads are broken away from the source in a quick, snapping motion.

All these different approaches are used to accomplish the same thing, that is, harvest the crop. **The method selected depends upon the type of fruit or vegetable to be harvested, not the skills, nor desires of the person who will be doing the harvesting.** The important thing is the accomplishment, not the method used.

> *"...open your eyes, and look at the fields; they are ripe for harvest." John 4:35*

There are many, many people in the world today who are ripe for the harvest. They believe in God, but they are not born again. They" believe in God, but...." These "buts" fall into five general categories. Let's take a look at them.

"I BELIEVE IN GOD, BUT..."

"I DON'T BELIEVE HE IS A PERSONAL GOD...."

Typical Statement. *"I believe that God is the great creator and great overseer of the universe. He keeps the universe in order, He allows things to happen then by chance, as they will. I believe there is life after death, and that God will judge every person according to the sum of his life – balancing the good against the bad on His divine scales, and then reward accordingly."*

Now that is really interesting. Where do you suppose they got this idea? Where is their authority for this type of thinking? It has to be something conjured up within their finite minds, reasoning from a concept of fairness.

True, God is the great creator and great overseer, but He also knows each living individual (and hasn't forgotten the dead ones). In fact, God is such a personal God that He knows more about you than you know about yourself.

Jesus said, **" Are not five sparrows sold for two pennies? Yet not one of them is forgotten by God. Indeed, the very hairs of your head are all numbered. Don't be afraid, you are worth more than many sparrows."** Luke 12:6-7

And even more important than His knowledge about your external characteristics, Luke 16:15 says "... **God knows your hearts...**" He reads your intents, motives, and desires. Is there anything more personal than that?

"I DON'T BELIEVE THE BIBLE IS THE WORD OF GOD..."

Typical Statement. *" I believe the Bible is a collection of history books, and stories, and rules, put together by the Hebrew nation and added to by others later. If the Bible is God's Word, why was it written? There is no proof that the Bible is God's Word."*

Hold on. Proof is simple enough for those who need it and who will be reasonable. The Bible contains many, and I emphasize many, prophecies that were made years and hundreds of years before their literal fulfillment.

Question: What are the mathematical odds of prophesying one event, just one, correctly simply one year from now?

Consider the 22nd Psalm. There are over a dozen prophecies in this chapter alone, written not one year before the event, but 1,000 years before the event. These were specifically and literally fulfilled on the day of Jesus crucifixion. The mathematical odds of these happening multiplies by geometrical progression until they virtually approach infinity. Only God could have been responsible for this.

*But the Bible says, **"The just shall live by faith"** —not proof. Faith means believe, and believe means accept.*

Why was the Bible written? The Bible itself gives that answer.

"But these are written that you may believe that Jesus is the Christ, the Son of God; and that by believing you may have life in his name." *John 20:31*

I DON'T BELIEVE THAT JESUS CHRIST WAS THE SON OF GOD

Typical Statement. *I'll agree that Jesus was a good man and a remarkable teacher, but Son of God? I can't believe that."* Jesus said, **"Do not let your hearts be troubled. Trust in God, trust also in me."** *John 14:1*

When Jesus was baptized at the Jordan River by John the Baptist, a voice came out of heaven saying, **"This is my Son whom I love; with him I am well pleased."** *Matt 3:17. Whose voice could it have been, but God's?*

Jesus also said, **"Believe me when I say that I am in the Father, and the Father is in me: or at least believe on the evidence of the miracles themselves."** *John 14:11 The reference to the Father is an unmistakable reference to God. This statement brings us to the crux of the matter. If Jesus was not the Son of God, then He was insane. Insane people can gather followers. Insane people can attract crowds to listen – Hitler did. But, insane men don't walk on water; insane men don't change water into wine; insane men don't heal leprosy, blindness, and lameness. Those miracles were God's stamp of authenticity upon Jesus, His Son. And Jesus appealed to those well-documented miracles for a catalyst and springboard to launch a doubting soul into hurling his trust and belief in Him.*

I DON'T BELIEVE THAT JESUS DIED FOR OUR SIN...

Typical Statement. *"Perhaps Jesus was the Son of God, sent here to teach us moral and ethical principles, and how to live a wholesome life, but I can't believe He had **to die for my sin**. That is dirty, messy, bloody, and barbaric. Unnecessary! The thought of God requiring a blood sacrifice is repugnant. Jesus' death by crucifixion was just an unfortunate mistake."*

If the reader feels he will have trouble thrusting his sickle into this objection, a re-reading of the chapters FOUR SEASONS and THE DAY THE LAMB DIED is suggested.

I DON'T BELIEVE JESUS CHRIST LIVES TODAY.

Typical Statement: *"I don't believe the resurrection. It is either a myth, a delusion, a conspiracy, or a misunderstanding."*

Many people do not believe that Jesus rose again from the grave, physically and literally, and lives today. But the Bible makes this point unmistakably clear. Jesus physically appeared to too many people for all of them to be deluded. History records that all twelve disciples (Matthias substituted for Judas) died a violent death on behalf of Jesus.

Do men voluntarily die for a lie?

The resurrection is the core of the Gospel.

The Bible relates that the disciples were not quick to believe in the resurrection. One, Thomas, demanded satisfaction of his physical senses: sight, sound, and touch --three powerful senses. Furthermore, Jesus' opponents were confounded by the event and were never able to prove that He did not live – and you can be sure, if such proof were possible, it would have come forth.

There are many people, even within the church world, who quietly reject Jesus' resurrection. They suggest that it is the "spirit" of Jesus that lives on today. By compromising in this fashion, they can relieve themselves of the absurdity of believing in a total, physical resurrection. But Jesus Himself said He would live again after three days. It had to happen to put God's stamp of TRUTH on the entire redemptive process.

> *"The harvest is truly plenteous, but the laborers are few." Matt. 9:37*

One of the saddest things about Christianity in America is the general apathy of born-again Christians concerning the multitude of unbelievers. The Bible verse above virtually screams out its truth.

Among the many reasons for apathy, there seem to be two that are universal.

First, many Christians who are not in full-time service feel insignificant. They see the great Gospel crusades and all the activity of the evangelists and preachers working in the fields and feel there is not much they can do that is not already being done on a bigger and grander scale.

Of course, this is indeed a mistake. They have failed to realize that some of the sweetest fruit comes out of the garden and orchard harvested one by one, by hand, individually.

Second, they feel inadequate and unprepared. They have never been taught to be fishers of men. They have never been taught how to 'win souls.' Here, they fail to realize there doesn't have to be a formal, professional preparation – indeed, it very possibly could be a detriment. What is 'being prepared?'

Let's go back to the garden and orchard. Someone who has never been in a garden certainly doesn't need much help or instruction on how to gather the harvest. And whatever instruction he does need, is best learned 'on the job.' The five methods of harvest (pick up, pull out, pick off, cut off, and snap off) are natural. A person doesn't even have to stop and think, "Now, how will I get this?" No, he just goes ahead and does it. Naturally. Orchard and garden harvest is more a matter of being in the right place at the right time and being willing to work.

And so is harvesting for Jesus Christ. It is a matter of being willing to work and being in the right place at the right time. In this realm, there are also five elements involved in the harvest: **The Word, Prayer, Faith, Testimony, and Life.**

The Word. *Read the Bible faithfully and continually and know where key verses can be found. The Gospel of John, alone, has enough in it to lead any man to salvation.*

Prayer *is like plugging the power cord into the socket or power source. Communing with God, letting the love flow back and forth, prayer prepares the soul for the work ahead.*

Faith *is often overlooked. Believe that God will lead you to the right place at the right time, and give you the thoughts and words that He wants you to use. You will find it will happen as you claim it.*

Speak out for Jesus *when the opportunity presents itself. If you don't know what to say, just tell what He has done for you and how He did it. Just tell it like it is. Please, don't glamorize or embellish it. Simply tell how Jesus saved you and gave you peace, joy, love, and eternal life. If the situation seems right, ask your listener if he has been born again. Then listen! If the answer is "no," invariably your listener will continue on to tell you why. Let him talk it out, then* **answer** *– not* **argue.** *Use the Word as best you can, and don't become frustrated. God has given you this opportunity in His wisdom – let Him guide and direct you. When you feel it appropriate (not if)* **invite** *your listener to accept Jesus Christ as his personal savior.*

Pray with him *right there. He will probably not know what to say. Tell him to ask Jesus to forgive him of all his sins, and to come into his heart to cleanse him and live there* forever. After that, just praise the Lord and keep on praising the Lord.

Your Life. This is the only element left. No matter how powerful your testimony is, it will be nullified if your life does not reflect the love of God working in you. A breakdown on your part, in reading the Word, in your prayer life, and in your faith, will immediately be reflected in your life. How many times has this happened to me! The record of my life seems worse than that of Israel, wandering for forty years after being saved. To be sure, our salvation does not depend upon our performance—but someone else's might! If your life is inconsistent, you might do more harm than good on the harvest field.

> **"As a prisoner for the Lord, then, I urge you to live a life worthy of the calling you have received. Be completely humble and gentle; be patient, bearing with one another in love. Make every effort to keep the unity of the Spirit through the bond of peace."** *Ephesians 4:1-3*

In summary:

> **"Whatever you do, work at it with all your heart, as working for the Lord, not for men,"** *Colossians 3:23*

CHAPTER TWENTY FIVE

Fire Flies

Tiny flickers of illumination

On two recorded occasions, Jesus told his disciples to "consider" living objects of nature. The verb, "consider " in the sense He used it means to perceive and learn thoroughly with the mind, the significant action or attribute of the object in focus. In Luke 12:24-27, Jesus told His disciples to consider the ravens and the lilies.

Close observation of nature at work and play will reveal to the observer many truths and the magnificence of the wisdom of God. Here are a few observations this author has made. We call them Fire Flies (from whence came the title of this book) because they are little flickers of heavenly-sent illuminations.

Consider the Great Blue Heron...

One of my wife's favorite pastimes is to watch the Great Blue Heron. Regardless of what she is doing, when she sees that regal bird sweep into one of our ponds, she runs for the binoculars. This graceful creature, a full four feet in height, stands in the shallow water like a stone statue for incredibly long periods of time. His virtue....**patience.** He is waiting for his dinner, indeed, his dinner depends upon his patience.

Christians should pray constantly for patience. It is a necessary ingredient to heavenly fruit production. The Apostle Paul ranked patience with godliness, faith, love, righteousness, and meekness. I Timothy 6:11

Although totally motionless, the heron is not asleep. Quite the contrary, he is alert and vigilant. Eventually, quick as a lightening bolt, his head darts into the water and comes up with a fish. He was ready for the opportunity that presented itself.

The Apostle Peter said, "...always be prepared to give an answer to everyone who asks you to give the reason for the hope that you have..." I Peter 3:15

Consider the juice apples...

They must be broken and crushed to produce the cider. Juice apples cannot accomplish their ultimate goal until they are put through the grinder and the press – crushed to yield their very living fluids.

Jesus was broken and crushed for us. The 53rd chapter of Isaiah prophesies how he would be stricken, smitten, wounded, and bruised. That latter word means to crush, to break, to kill, to die. Jesus yielded His very life blood on the Cross to accomplish the ultimate goal – that of salvation for all men.

Occasionally Christians are crushed and broken for Christ's sake. Jesus said, " **The servant is not greater than his Lord...**" *John 13:16. Some have experienced martyrdom. Others have been crushed and broken and left in this world – their lives shattered by the loss of their families and loved ones, their businesses, their properties, and virtually everything. Some of the sweetest Christians are such as these who have suffered for Christ's sake. Their testimonies are powerful and fruitful, as they keep their eyes on Jesus* *and give Him the glory of their faith and trust.*

But also consider – once crushed, if the cider is **not used**, it hardens and becomes intoxicating, eventually turning to vinegar. This lesson is obvious.

Consider the volunteer plant....

It is usually the first one up in the springtime and grows with vigor. It is invariably one of the largest, hardiest, and first to fruit. A volunteer is one who wants to grow and offers to bloom. He brings forth much fruit. There is an old chorus…. "A volunteer for Jesus…"

Consider the cow....

Folks often enjoy watching cows being bred artificially. There seems to be fascination concerning the ability and technique of impregnating an animal with the seed of another animal that is perhaps thousands of miles away, or even dead. Taking the semen out of the liquid nitrogen, thawing it, breaking the capsule, drawing the viscose liquid up into a pipette, and inserting the pipette for delivery, are all points of interest. But they really don't amount to much, for in breeding a cow, it is not what happens on the **outside** that is important, but that which happens on the **inside**. The critical work of the breeder is the internal placement of the pipette in the proper spot for delivery of the semen. Whether or not she conceives, depends in large part on this inward work. In due time, if she conceives, there is outward evidence of this inward work.

Is this not a picture of the new creature in Jesus Christ?

Consider the fruit tree....

Most do not bear fruit for the first couple of years after being set out. It takes a certain amount of time for the tree to become established, rooted, strong, to gain growth, and become mature enough to fruit.

Sometimes older, mature Christians fall into the trap of "judging" new converts, and have forgotten the lesson of the fruit tree. New converts don't need to be judged, they need to be cultivated. They don't need to be criticized, they need to be watered. They don't need to be purged, they need to be fed. In due time the fruit will appear. They need to be encouraged, not discouraged.

Consider the lamb....

Have you ever observed a lamb nursing? When a lamb sucks its mother, it gets down on its front knees. The lamb gets down on its knees to make contact with its source of life.

This is a perfect, God-given example for Christians. Our source of eternal life is our Lord Jesus. We make contact with Him, are sustained and refreshed by Him, while on our knees – in prayer.

The Bible has numerous references to the bent knee in prayer and worship in a literal sense. It is a preferred position, not a required one. However, in this example, the emphasis seems to lie, not in the bodily position, but in making contact with the source of life. In this sense, bent knees suggest humility, obedience, and a subservient, submissive, inward position.

Consider the grapevine....

Its long arms can be trained to grow into any pattern that it is set and secured. Once trained into position, it will remain for its entire lifetime. Surely the vine needs regular pruning and the dead wood needs to be cut off, but the trunk and main limbs are set into place.

> *"Train a child in the way he should go: and when he is old, he will not turn from it."*
> Proverbs 22:6

Consider pigs...

Mature hogs, if allowed to gain weight, become lazy just lying around all day doing nothing. There is an observable truth in the old expression, "...fat and lazy as a pig." But young growing hogs are another story. They do lie around and sleep a great deal, but they are also extremely excitable, especially at feeding time. When a herd of hogs become aware of the presence of a person, they will often become still and motionless, but very alert as they watch the person approach. Then, invariably, one hog will snort, and the entire herd will commence running at break-neck speed. They bring to mind the account of Jesus allowing the demons to enter the swine that is found in all three Synoptic Gospels.

When hogs are allowed to run free, they can cause incredible damage, virtually wrecking havoc wherever they choose. They have gotten into our barn on occasion. They deliberately knock over buckets and machinery, trample plants, root up worm beds, tear open sacks of cement, knock down tools they can reach, and strew trash all over. The bottom line is **they respect nothing**.

> "*...do not throw your pearls to pigs, if you do, they may trample them under their feet, and then turn and tear you to pieces.*" Matt. 7:6b

Consider the flower bulb...

...tulips, dahlias, iris, lilies, etc. They multiply by dividing. **God's arithmetic!** Who can fathom the wisdom of God? Indeed, multiplying by dividing.

This brings to mind Paul and Barnabas who traveled together on their first missionary journey. When they prepared for their second missionary trip, as related in Acts 15, sharp contention arose between them, and they chose separate companions and departed in different directions. Net result: two missionary teams instead of one! But can't you just hear the gossips in Antioch...?"

"Tsk, tsk, have you heard about Paul and Barnabas? Oh, my, what a shame! They've had a falling out over John Mark, and even got to shouting at each other. So sad. Now they have split up. Can't be God's Will..."

Who can discern the mind of God?
People often wonder why there are so many churches of different denominations. Skeptics point to this fact in an attempt to discredit the message of the Church. Others refer to this inability of the churches to agree as if it invalidates God's gift.

Has not God divided the bulb to multiply the blossoms?

Consider the new calf...

...who becomes infected soon after birth by germs from dirt that enters through the still exposed, raw navel cord. The baby contracts "joint-ill" – a nasty disease of pus and infection in its joints. Sometimes it is fatal, invariably it is crippling for life. The calf's ability to walk is severely impaired. He limps, he hobbles, and staggers in frustration and pain. He can never live a normal life, for he was ruined shortly after birth.

The Bible points out in numerous places that the ability to walk spiritually is critical. II Corinthians 5:7 **"We live by faith, not by sight..."** *Ephesians 4:1* **" ...live a life worthy of the calling you have received..."** *Colossians 1:10* **"...live a life worthy of the Lord..."** *and I John 1:7* **" But if we walk in the light, as he is in the light, we have fellowship with one another, and the blood of Jesus, his Son, purifies us from all sin."**

Woe unto pastors and teachers who infect new believers with spiritual joint-ill by misleading them into error, by wrongly dividing the Word of Truth. They will be held accountable before God.

Consider the rainfall and snowfall...
Consider how tons of water, either liquid or solid, can be dumped from the sky in a short period of time onto a small plot of ground, without hurting so much as a blade of grass.
Isn't God's wisdom remarkable?

So many examples, so little time...
There are so many of God's creatures and so much of God's creation "to consider" in the light of Biblical teaching. The list could go on and on ad infinitum. From the humming bird to the eagle, from the tiny wild flower to the towering pine tree, from the honey bee to the draft horse.

The ultimate consciousness of God's world around us and His lessons to us involves a three-step progression. Each step builds upon the previous one. Unfortunately, most folks in today's world never even take the first step. Our society lives in preoccupation. They are preoccupied with their businesses, they are preoccupied with their plans, they are preoccupied with "things" that are manufactured by humans.

Awareness
The first step in this unfolding consciousness is awareness. Before one can appreciate, one must become aware. One must see, one must hear, one must touch. Just a few minutes ago, my wife and my daughter came by my office and asked me to join them for a swim in our lake. As it was incredibly hot and also the first day of summer vacation for them, I consented. We had a wonderful time. We paddled around in the boat, jumped out and swam, played splash, and generally enjoyed a refreshing time together. But the entire experience was enriched by my wife's extraordinary awareness to her surroundings that she shared with us. She spotted a thistle seed "walking on the water" – a round

multi-spiked fluff object being blown across the surface that actually looked like it was walking. She called our attention to a beautiful yellow-orange bird that invaded the red-winged blackbird's tree on the island and got chased away in a hurry. Schools of tiny, miniature fish darted together, first in one direction, and then another. Just so much life is in evidence around a body of water.

Sensitivity

The second step is sensitivity – receiving impressions and responding to the external stimulus. Alertness. Pre-occupation looks, but does not see. Awareness looks and sees, but does not observe. Sensitivity looks, sees, and observes. Pre-occupation hears noise, whereas awareness hears sounds. But sensitivity hears sounds and listens – indeed, studies God's creation as it is – and to study is to learn.

Application

The last step. This one exemplifies the admonition of Jesus – *"Consider..."* He is saying – be aware, be sensitive, learn the lessons of nature as they apply to both our spiritual and physical lives here on earth. Perceive the wisdom and omniscience of God who designed His creation so rich and full of marvelous examples of His plan and purpose for mankind.

God bless you

Printed in the United States
23605LVS00002B/82-510